A BRIEF HISTORY OF

THE HOLY GRAIL

GILES MORGAN

ROBINSON

RUNNING PRESS
PHILADELPHIA · LONDON

Constable & Robinson Ltd
3 The Lanchesters
162 Fulham Palace Road
London W6 9ER
www.constablerobinson.com

First published in the UK by Robinson,
an imprint of Constable & Robinson Ltd, 2011

A copy of the British Library Cataloguing in
Publication Data is available from the British Library

ISBN: 978-1-84901-411-3

1 3 5 7 9 10 8 6 4 2

First published in the United States in 2011 by Running Press Book Publishers

9   8   7   6   5   4   3   2   1
Digit on the right indicates the number of this printing

Library of Congress Control Number: 2010928997
US ISBN: 978-0-7624-4101-3

Running Press Book Publishers
2300 Chestnut Street
Philadelphia, PA 19103-4371
www.runningpress.com

Visit us on the web!
www.runningpress.com

Printed and bound in the EU

CONTENTS

CHAPTER THREE: GLASTONBURY AND THE GRAIL

CHAPTER FOUR: ARTHUR AND THE HOLY GRAIL

CHAPTER FIVE: GRAIL MYSTERIES

CHAPTER SIX: THE GRAIL REVIVAL

The Holy Grail
in Britain and
Europe

Rosslyn
Chapel

Wroxeter

Nanteos

Caerleon

Glastonbury
Tintagel   South Cadbury

Dozmary Pool

Turin

Rennes-le-Chateau

Montségur

INTRODUCTION

For all its iconic properties there remains something fundamentally elusive about the subject of the Holy Grail. An
enigma wrapped within a mystery, it seems at times to move
out of reach when approached by the quester, the visionary or
simply the curious. As immediately recognisable as the figures
of King Arthur, Merlin and the Knights of the Round Table,
with whom it has come to be identified, it nonetheless
confounds expectation and presumption on closer analysis.
The roots of a Grail tradition can be found deep in ancient
Western history but can also be found to contain elements of
Eastern mysticism. It has in turn been an object of reverence,
devotion, yearning and a powerful tool for political and religious propaganda.

It can be seen to possess a mirror-like quality as it reflects
the people and belief systems that have incorporated it into
their worldview. The complexity of its origins is matched by
its enduring appeal as a metaphor for quest, struggle, ultimate
achievement and sometimes painfully, ultimate failure. Unpicking
the strands of its development is a telling account of the dreams
and ambitions of humanity, its triumphs, obsessions and
darkest cruelties. But the Grail does not merely belong to the

past as a redundant artefact of antiquity; its tradition is alive and evolving in the modern world.

The French poet Chrétien de Troyes from Champagne was instrumental in crystallising the story of the Grail as we know it today. Working between around 1170 to 1190 he produced a series of romances which drew heavily on the British Arthurian tales. The immense popularity of King Arthur in the medieval period is borne out by the fact that no less a figure than Richard the Lionheart himself christened his own sword Excalibur. Whether this might be construed as what we would call today an attempt at 'spin' or reflected an ardent belief in the values which Arthur seemed to enshrine, it is difficult to gauge. Nonetheless it indicates clearly that they were powerful stories and myths that would have been known at all levels of society.

De Troyes introduced the symbol of the Grail in his final tale *Conte del Graal* or 'story of the grail'. It introduces the idea of a physical and spiritual quest to the court of King Arthur. A Welsh youth called Perceval undertakes a series of adventures in his quest to become a knight of Arthur's court, in one of which he meets a mysterious Fisher King and encounters the Grail at his castle. The Fisher King has been wounded or crippled and makes a gift of a sword to Perceval. At this point the Grail Procession enters the castle. The procession is made up of a young man bearing a 'bleeding' lance, a young woman carrying a shining Grail made of precious materials and a maiden with a carving dish. Through the asking of a ritual question the Grail has the power to heal the king and his kingdom, the 'wasteland', which has been directly affected by his injury. Perceval fails to ask the question and, after he later realises his failure, he devotes the rest of his life to finding the Grail. This also precipitates later quests by other knights.

At this point the Grail is not a specifically Christian artefact and the story remained unfinished at the time of Chrétien's death. It is possible to find many parallels between this story and Celtic Arthurian stories. Both the Christian and the pre-Christian versions contain a dream-like quality in which they seem to function on the level of pure symbolism. In this sense they represent an encoded, unfolding mystery tradition.

The Holy Grail becomes an explicitly Christian symbol in Robert de Boron's *Joseph of Arimathea*, which appeared in about 1190. Here it is specifically described as the cup of the Last Supper and the chalice in which Christ's blood is caught by Joseph of Arimathea. But de Boron was at this point adding to an already existing storytelling tradition, which dated back to pre-Christian Celtic cultures and beyond. The body of literature, which has come to be known as the Matter of Britain, combines Celtic mythology and the Arthurian tales with the Grail, matching the development of Christianity in Britain and Europe. Joseph of Arimathea is said to have brought the Grail to Glastonbury and established the first Christian church in Britain. The Grail becomes a symbol of Celtic Christianity, fusing pagan beliefs with the new religion brought from the Middle East.

In Celtic mythology the Grail has parallels with other magical vessels, like the magic cauldron which makes many appearances in tales such as 'The Spoils of Annwn', collected in the Mabinogion. Significantly, it can bring the dead back to life and provide limitless food, echoing many of the properties later said to be possessed by the Grail. The sacred vessel, such as the Greek cup of Dionysos, provider of inspiration, and the cauldron of the Dagda, an ancient Irish god who owned a cauldron of plenty, can be found in many world religions and cultures. The cauldron can be seen as a central motif of shamanic cultures and their associated ritual ceremonies. Illustrative mouldings on the Gunderstrup cauldron dating from 1st or 2nd century BC Denmark appear to show an antlered God surrounded by animals and it has been suggested that this could represent a shamanic figure communicating with the spirits of the natural world. By creating hallucinogenic mixtures many shamanic cultures attempt to gain supernatural skills and abilities and the role of the cauldron in this process is both practical and symbolic. The Gunderstrup cauldron also shows a depiction of dead warriors who may be waiting to be brought back to life by the horned god Cernunnos. By dipping them head first in his cauldron they can be re-born. The recurring theme of re-birth in pagan and Christian cultures is a powerful one.

During the medieval period the Grail became closely associated with both the Cathars and the Templars. Both groups were Christian in origin but developed dissenting belief systems which drew on heretical sources such as the teachings of the Gnostics and contained elements of Eastern mysticism. Many stories link the Cathars and the Grail and the Templars have been seen as its guardians. Both suffered terrible persecution by the orthodox church and many theories have developed around their relationship to the Grail. It has been variously argued that the Grail is, in fact, the container holding the Turin Shroud, of which the Templars were at one point the guardians, and that the Holy Grail may actually represent a Holy Bloodline descended directly from Christ. Interest has centred on Rosslyn chapel in Scotland where some believe an actual Grail found its resting place as the Templars fled persecution in Europe.

In 1207 Wolfram von Eschenbach produced *Parzival*, a text in which the Grail takes the form of a stone and not the established symbol of the cup. His version of the Grail story contains many Eastern influences and incorporates many ideas found in alchemy. This reflects the meeting of cultures which came about during the time of the crusades and indicates a cross-pollination of ideas emerging from a background of religious war.

During the 18th and 19th centuries there was a major revival in interest in the medieval period and the Grail Quests of the Arthurian romances became a major source of inspiration for new generations of artists, writers and composers. It featured in the work of the Pre-Raphaelites, William Blake, Tennyson, Aubrey Beardsley and became the basis of Richard Wagner's *Parsifal*.

The fascination with the Grail intensified in the 20th century as it found expression and interpretation in a wide range of cultural forms and ideas. The poet T. S. Eliot bases much of his groundbreaking poem *The Waste Land* on the Grail stories and epic story tellers like T. H. White and Tolkien continue the tradition of adopting elements of earlier texts to produce their own mythologies. Mythograhers like Joseph Campbell wrote extensively on the subject and it became an important universal symbol for the psychologist Carl Jung and his wife.

On a more disturbing level the Grail story of Wagner's *Parsifal* became an inspiration for Adolf Hitler and the themes of Grail quest were twisted and appropriated by the Nazi party. It is known that Hitler's interest in the occult and mythology included a fascination with ancient artefacts. In this sense the Grail can be seen to be symbolic on a darker level of obsession and mania as well as in its more positive aspects of quest, struggle, healing and renewal.

It has proved influential in film making from the sublime, such as John Boorman's *Excalibur*, to the ridiculous in the satire of Monty Python's *Holy Grail*. In the films of Steven Spielberg and George Lucas the Grail tradition has provided both an implicit and explicit template for storytelling and at the beginning of a new century the cycle comes full circle with the current *Lord of the Rings* trilogy.

The Holy Grail is a potent and compelling image in the modern psyche and its continued evolution is proof of its incredible symbolic flexibility. We have come to understand the quest for the Holy Grail as being representative of personal struggle, collective journeying and as ultimate achievement in all areas of human endeavour. That the most popular Western films of today contain elements reaching back as far as pre-history may represent an unexpected surprise but also an affirmation of the cyclical nature of human existence and culture.

THE HOLY GRAIL

I

THE MAGICAL VESSEL

Pre-Christian Sources

The Holy Grail has come to be seen today as a specifically Christian symbol. Through the medieval romances of the 12th century and onwards it is described as the cup used by Christ himself at the Last Supper and the same vessel in which Joseph of Arimathea caught the blood of Christ. In many accounts of the Christian Grail it is viewed as having regenerative, healing and nourishing qualities, both spiritually and physically. Details surrounding the Christian Grail can be seen to change in different accounts of the story, which are discussed in more detail in later chapters, but these are the basic ideas associated with it.

However, the concept of the Sacred Vessel carrying high cultural status and associations with renewal and regeneration can be found in a plethora of sources in the Pre-Christian period. Indeed parallels can be drawn in a wide range of world-wide cultures where recurrent motifs and ideas are echoed in later versions of the Grail story. As we shall see it is the universal elements of the Grail tradition which have contributed to its enduring appeal and success throughout history. Drawing on popular existing stories and traditions, which often enshrined ancient beliefs and ideas, poets and writers of the medieval period Christianised the Grail.

In order to gain insight into the rich myths of the Grail it is necessary to look back into our remote past where so many of the aspects of its later form have their beginnings. During the period known as the Neolithic, or new Stone Age, European human culture was undergoing great changes. The established system of survival of the hunter-gatherers whose nomadic habits go back to the earliest of human origins was giving way to a more settled agrarian lifestyle. Small family or community groups were farming the land and slowly gaining greater control over their food supplies and collective destinies. This socio-economic revolution had important repercussions for the values and belief systems of the people of this period. The new approach to life seems to have brought its own anxieties and responsibilities, which found their expression in the great Megalithic structures that include West Kennet Long Barrow and Avebury stone circle of Wiltshire in England.

There seems to have been a growing obsession with the fertility of both the land and the people themselves. The great stones of Avebury have been interpreted as having sexualised forms. Tall phallic stones are interspersed with 'broad-hipped' stones that have a fuller shape reminiscent of the female form. At the same time there is an emergence or an increased focus on the importance of ancestral veneration expressed in the interment of bones at sites such as West Kennet Long Barrow, which become important centres for ritual. The underlying concern is with the success of crops and the fertility of their animals and themselves. The symbolism of the cornucopia or horn of plenty overflowing with fruit or corn has its roots in this. Ancestors are seen as providing an important link between the living and the forces of nature, which may have been symbolised as individual deities.

There seems to have been a general trend for the collective interment of bones during the Neolithic period which suggests that power resided in groups of people, perhaps important families.

At this point in history the Great Mother Goddess of the earth seems to have been a dominating influence, as is shown by the often womb-like forms that burial chambers of this period take and the proximity of sites such as Callanish in Scotland to hill forms which are often viewed as recumbent goddess figures.

The trend towards important burials of individuals with high status grave goods emerges during the Bronze Age (2200–700 BC) which suggests that power was shifting from collective groups or families towards a single, high-status figure. Grave goods, such as a beaker at the West Kennet Long Barrow, have been found in early burial sites, suggesting a belief in an after-life or an Otherworld in which the vessel will be used by the dead. During the Bronze Age cups were commonly placed in graves. These were made principally from pottery, sometimes amber and, much more rarely, gold. A recent example is the cup found at Ringlemere in Kent in a Bronze Age Barrow. Dating from 1700–1500 BC, it is thought to have been a ritual offering to an important local leader. It has been beaten from a single lump of gold and shows evidence of a high degree of metalwork-ing skill. Cups placed with the dead may have been intended for drinking alcohol in the form of mead or beer and this could reflect the importance of group feasting in building loyalties and close ties. Certainly cups were seen as just as important objects as weapons like swords, axes and daggers.

World Mythologies
The image of a container or vessel with sacred or otherworldly connotations can be found throughout different world mythol-ogies. Though details and contexts may vary, basic elements of storytelling and symbolism emerge time after time. Greek myth provides numerous stories that feature just such magical objects. Medea the witch who assists Jason in his search for the golden fleece has a cauldron of re-birth which she demon-strates by cutting up an old sheep and drawing out a living lamb. The significant and parallel elements of the tale to the

Grail tradition are the matching themes of the quest and the magical vessel. Like the later Grail Knights, Jason must face many trials and obstacles to achieve his goal.

Plato used the image of the Greek Krater, a vessel for mixing concentrated wine with water, as a metaphor for the creation of the universe. Through the mixing of different elements in this transformative cup, life is created by the deity. The god Dionysos provides humanity with inspiration from his cup.

In another myth Hades, the underworld god, offers the goddess Persephone a cup containing pomegranate seeds. Upon eating six seeds she is forced to live in the underworld with Hades. However, her mother Demeter makes an agreement with Hades to allow her daughter to return to earth for half the year. (This echoes later stories about making pacts with the Christian devil.)

Upon Persephone's annual return the land, which has been laid waste through sorrow for her absence, is rejuvenated and comes to life again. This story represents ancient concerns with the cycle of the seasons, the yearly process of vegetative death and renewal and the inter-relationship of these seasons as personified in the form of gods and goddesses. It also looks forward to the later Grail stories where achievement of the chalice cup allows the barren wasteland to flower again. The motif of the magic cup recurs again in one of the tales featuring the Greek hero Hercules. In this instance, in order to steal cattle from Geryoneus who lives on the island of Erytheia, Hercules borrows the giant gold cup of Helios the sun god to reach his destination. Helios used the cup for his own evening journey across the ocean to return to the east. In this combined image Hercules can be seen as representing both a quester and, in conjunction with the life-giving properties of the sun, a figure of strength and fertility. The use of the cup in obtaining cattle finds echoes in the abundance and plenty offered by later Grail myths.

An important and widespread myth of the Celtic people of the British Isles about the sun has similar features to the journey of Helios. Every day, upon its setting in the west, the sun would be carried in a boat through the underworld, ready to re-appear the next day in the east. Numerous themes of cup/boat symbolism emerge in this story, which will find later resonance in the mythology of the Grail. The magical vessel of re-birth and renewal is married with the theme of a voyage to an Otherworld. In the Arthurian legends the King, after his death, is carried by boat to the mysterious isle of Avalon in the West. In some versions of the story, Arthur is laid to rest in a cave, ready for the time when he is needed again by Britain. Details vary but the recurrent image is of re-birth and of Arthur waiting to become King once again.

In ancient Egypt we find the image of the magical, life-giving container in connection with the goddess Satet. Her name has been recorded on tomb inscriptions dating from 2289 to 2255 BC. Satet is connected with the yearly flooding of the river Nile, the season known as 'akhet', the inundation. Heavy rains during the summer months between June and September in the Ethiopian highlands result in the flooding of the river that brings with it both water and precious fertilising silt. Each year the goddess Isis was said to shed a single tear on the 'night of the teardrop' which Satet would catch in her jars and pour into the Nile. She is described as having four vases and has the power to purify the dead with her water and assist in their re-birth in the afterlife. In this sense she is both a Water Goddess and a fertility deity, the two aspects being complimentary to the whole. A temple was built in dedication to her on Elephantine Island in the Nile. This is one of the first points the floodwater reaches and was measured by a 'Nileometer', a depth measure cut into stone on the riverbank.

In other cultures throughout the world, the cup is of importance in religion and mythology. In Tibet the transience of life and the decay and death of the human body is symbolised by the Tibetan skull cup. A Tibetan goddess is sometimes depicted drinking from a skull cup, and it is used in religious ceremonies. It has the power to transform as the dead move to different levels of consciousness through her regenerative powers.

In this context, the Inuit people of Greenland have an intriguing myth about the Northern Lights or Aurora Borealis. It was believed that the spirits of the dead, playing a game with a walrus skull, created the flickering curtain of coloured lights. The dead want to join the living and anyone who sees the light should give a low whistle to acknowledge them. Here the animal skull becomes a bridge between the two worlds of the living and the dead just as the Christian Grail links the earthly realm with the divine and heaven.

Norse culture contains many references to magical vessels and the equally powerful brews that they are said to contain. The home of the Norse gods was Asgard, which was originally inhabited by a group of deities called the Vanir. When a rival group, the Aesir, came to Asgard they began a war against the more peaceable Vanir. Eventually a truce was called and finalised by the assembled gods spitting into a bowl. A new god springs from the bowl, Kvasir, who becomes the god of wisdom.

Odin, an Aesir god, is connected with Kvasir through the mead of inspiration. This magical brew is created when Kvasir is murdered by two dwarves and his blood drained and mixed with honey and left to ferment. Significantly they catch his blood in two jars called Son, meaning 'truth' and Bodn, meaning 'offering' or 'prayer'. They mix it in a cauldron called Odrorir. This can be translated as both 'inspiration' and 'furiously roaring'. Odin, who is known as a wanderer with a thirst for knowledge, sets out on a journey to drink this special brew. After a series of adventures in which Odin shape-shifts into different forms, including an ordinary man and a snake, he drinks the mead which has been hidden in a cave by a giant. Fleeing in the form of an eagle, Odin returns to Asgard pursued by the giant who has also taken eagle form. The giant is killed when he flies into a fire lit by the other gods. Odin regurgitates the mead into vessels but spills some onto the earth. It is from these drops that poets are said to gain their inspiration.

Once again the theme of a dangerous quest is combined with the concept of the sacred vessel containing the blood of a deity, just as the chalice cup is said to contain the blood of Christ. The flowering of poetry through inspiration echoes the flowering of the land. As later chapters will show, the Grail has itself also proved a huge source of inspiration for poets and artists throughout history.

Shamanism

The figure of the shaman can be found in most ancient early cultures and shamanic practices have survived in some parts of the world right up to the present day. Derived from the Sanskrit word *sramana*, it means 'ascetic' or 'one who knows'. Commonly the shaman is a tribal figure who is able to travel to and communicate with an Otherworld in order to help his people and cure illness. The origins of shamanism may date back as far as 20–40,000 years. The role of the shaman is a combination of magician, healer, teacher and mystic. Examples of shamanic traditions can be found amongst the North American Indian tribes and in the indigenous peoples of South America.

Shamanism has been an important part of the religious practices of many other peoples, from Africa to Siberia, and has been present in the past cultures of many European countries. Very often the shaman reaches a state of ecstasy or trance through the ritual use of narcotics that allow him to move between the world of the living and the dead in order to assist individuals or the group or tribe. The role of the cup or cauldron in shamanic ritual in preparing sensory altering brews is likely to be an early model for the powers of the Christian Grail. Many Celtic myths concerning magic cauldrons may have their roots in shamanic ritual. The Gunderstrup cauldron dating from 1st or 2nd century BC Denmark depicts a horned god flanked by animals and some have interpreted him as a Celtic shaman communicating with nature spirits. Mind altering plants or fungi like the fly agaric (magic mushroom) contain psychoactive substances that can facilitate an out-of-body experience. The shaman can also reach his trance-like state through the repetitive beating of a drum or through ritual dancing. Other methods include singing, chanting, sleep deprivation and fasting. Turkish dervishes who spin to achieve different states of consciousness provide a related example of this technique.

The shaman journeys into spiritual Otherworlds to contact ancestral spirits, demons, gods or nature deities. Sometimes he assists in guiding the dying to the afterlife or battles the shamans of other tribes. His journey is often experienced as flying and shamans are sometimes said to have the power to change shape into animals and birds.

The Mabinogion
A series of Welsh myths and legends in prose form were collected together and translated by Lady Charlotte Guest during the 19th century and given the overall title of the Mabinogion. This translates as 'tales of youth' and concerns heroic deeds and feats often in connection with magical themes and a mysterious and magical Otherworld. They contain some of the first stories that feature King Arthur. They are amongst the earliest of recorded Celtic myths and formed an important basis for the Grail romances of later medieval writers such as Chrétien de Troyes. It is believed that they were written between approximately 1060 and 1250. The tales were originally written by more than one author and drew on an existing oral tradition. They combine pagan elements from Britain's past with Christian values and ideas.

However the representations of both the Grail and Arthur found here are quite different from the later more explicitly Christian prose cycles. In place of the chalice cup we find the recurrent image of the magic cauldron. The great poet Taliesin who is the Primary Chief Bard to the Island of Britain receives his skills and gifts from a magic cauldron. The cauldron belongs to Ceridwen, a Celtic fertility goddess particularly associated with the sow. In the story Ceridwen brews a potion for her disfigured son Avagddu, meaning darkness, which will provide him with knowledge and wisdom. Her servant Gwion is left to stir the cauldron although he is told not to drink from it. By accident three drops fly out and burn his finger. Without thinking he puts his finger into his mouth and gains huge wisdom.

This angers the goddess who pursues him. They both shape-shift several times. He becomes a hare and she a greyhound until eventually he transforms himself into a grain of wheat in a pile of grain. She transforms into a hen and pecks him out, swallowing the grain. She becomes pregnant and gives birth to the gifted bard and magician Taliesin. This is one example of tales from the Mabinogion which contain deities from a much older era and coded references to a shamanic tradition where insight is gained from hallucinatory drinks and the shaman is able to take on animal forms. There are also other stories in which the image of the magic cauldron appears. The figure of Bran the Blessed, for example, possesses a cauldron of re-birth in which dead warriors are brought back to life.

In the poem *Prieddeu Annwn*, 'the spoils of Annwn', Arthur travels to hell to gain a magic cauldron that has the power of re-birth and gives forth limitless food. When the dead are dipped headfirst into it they are miraculously brought back to life but are unable to speak. In this poem the cauldron of Annwn is kept in a 'revolving' castle and the image of the magically turning castle or island is found in many later Grail stories. Only seven of Arthur's company return from the journey – an echo of the difficulties and hardships of the Grail knights. Here then we have the pre-Christian Arthur linked to a quest to obtain a magic vessel housed in a mysterious fortress in which many of his men suffer and perish. The vessel has regenerative powers and is able magically to provide nourishment and plenty matching the properties of the later Grail.

Celtic Cauldron

In many ways the Celtic Cauldron as a cultural, physical and mythical object is the direct and immediate precursor to the Christian Grail. The term Celt comes from the Greek word 'Keltoi'. Indeed the majority of written information about the Celts comes from classical Greek or Roman sources. The term is something of a sweeping generalisation, used by the Greeks and Romans to describe a vast range of 'barbarian' peoples in central and Western Europe. The Celts described by classical writers such as Tacitus, Strabo, Julius Caesar and Pliny were the descendants of late Bronze Age peoples and, by extension, the farmers of the Neolithic period. They were, in many ways, widely differing people but they retained enough linguistic and cultural similarities to be identified by this broad term.

Iron Age Celtic culture emerges from archaeology, written sources and myths as a hierarchical one, based on a warrior elite with kings at the apex of the group. Feasting and the telling of tall tales seem to have been a focal point of much Celtic culture. They were primarily people with an oral tradition and this is typified by the training of their holy men, the druids, whom Caesar recorded as having a system of education which lasted as long as twenty years and involved the memorising of huge amounts of cultural and ritual knowledge. It is in this context that many of the elements of the first stories concerning King Arthur, Merlin and the Grail emerge.

As we have already seen, the cauldron is a common and important motif in Celtic storytelling. Indeed the Dagda, father of the Irish gods, has a cauldron of plenty that serves food to heroic warriors but which will not provide food for a coward. The cauldron as an image of re-birth, renewal, fertility and nourishment has strong links with water cults and examples of real Celtic cauldrons have been found in aquatic settings where it is believed they were placed as votive offerings. Examples of such offerings have been found at Llyn Cerrig Bach on the isle of Anglesey in a bog that would have been part of a lake during the Iron Age. Much of the metal work cast in as offerings consisted of weapons and accoutrements of war but also included cauldrons.

The practice of making such offerings was widespread during this period and further examples have been found in the Thames at Battersea, where an impressive shield was discovered, and at Waterloo, where a horned helmet had been cast into the river.

The great Gunderstrup cauldron itself had been dismantled and placed in a peat bog as a ritual offering. In around the 2nd or 3rd century BC a large bronze cauldron filled with over 2000 objects, also made of bronze, was placed in a natural spring called the 'Giant's springs' at Duchov in the Czech Republic as a sacred offering.

The practice of throwing prestigious weapons into lakes, rivers and springs to an otherworldly water deity finds echoes in the lady of the lake who gives Arthur his Otherworld sword, Excalibur, and to whom it is eventually returned.

In Ireland mythology tells of four magical objects that included the Cauldron of the Dagda. Brought to Ireland by a conquering race of Otherworld faery people called the Tuatha de Danaan, they served a symbolic function in Celtic culture. The other three items were the Stone of Destiny, the Spear of Lugh and the Sword of the Nuada.

These magical items form the basis for the symbols of the Cup, Spear, Stone and Dish, or the four hallows as they are called in the Grail stories.

2

THE CUP OF CHRIST

The Christian Grail

As we have seen, the concept of the magical vessel, sacred cup or receptacle is a widespread one. It is found in the earliest of human histories and the most basic model for it is provided by the human body itself. The roots of the Grail lie in the rich mythology of Celtic Europe in which a magic cauldron has strong associations with themes of nourishment, plenty, renewal and re-birth.

This potent image was to become intertwined through storytelling, both oral and written, with the equally legendary figure of King Arthur. Most historians agree that the real life Arthur was in all probability a Celtic chieftain or warlord from the centuries following the Roman withdrawal from Britain. He would have lived in approximately the 5th or 6th century AD. The earliest chroniclers of this period who were writing their histories several centuries later describe a divided Britain being overwhelmed by waves of Saxons and other incomers. Arthur appears to have been a figure who galvanised the Britons into fighting back and achieved some degree of success in halting this invasion. This success is demonstrated by the legends and myths that sprang up around him, often obscuring what factual detail remains. The Norman invasion of Britain served only to increase his popularity in folklore right across Europe. A frieze above the north doorway of Modena Cathedral in Italy depicts an Arthurian adventure and is significant because it has been dated as being produced between 1120 and 1140. This pre-dates the first of the French romances by several decades and points to his status as a well-known and recognisable figure at this time. Arthur is only found in Welsh texts previous to these dates and the most likely explanation for his fame lies in the storytelling traditions of the bards of Britain and Brittany.

The spread and growth of Christianity throughout Europe was to produce a fascination with a new miraculous vessel, the communion cup as used in the ritual of the Eucharist. For the early Christians the Eucharist or Holy Communion demonstrated an act of remembrance of Jesus Christ and also, importantly, was a communal rite that gave this persecuted group a sense of belonging and solidarity.

From around the 4th century onwards the role and meaning of the Eucharist was to develop and change quite radically and prove a major influence on the Grail romances of the 12th century. During the Eucharist bread and wine is consumed in remembrance of the Last Supper and Christ's suffering on the cross to redeem the sins of mankind.

A belief emerged through theological debate that the consecrated bread and wine actually became the body and blood of Christ. This miracle became known as transubstantiation and was to become an essential dramatic ritual at the very heart of the orthodoxy of the Roman Catholic Church. Eating the consecrated wafer and drinking from the consecrated chalice cup was a focus for great religious devotion in medieval society. The themes of Christ's sacrifice, death and re-birth and the promise of eternal life and salvation for Christians, which are central to this ritual, become in the French Arthurian romances the new template for the Grail.

The Matter of Britain

During the medieval period a large body of literature was produced, telling the history of Britain and King Arthur and his Knights, that has come to be referred to as 'the Matter of Britain'. In tracing the emergence of the Grail it is necessary to examine some of the major texts and authors in this body of work.

Geoffrey of Monmouth

The History of the Kings of Britain (in Latin, the *Historia Regum Britanniae*) was written by Geoffrey of Monmouth in 1136. It was to prove a very influential and popular work in the development of the Arthurian tales and, in many ways, reads more like a novel or a prose epic in the style of Homer's *Odyssey*, than like what would today be regarded as an historical account. It seems clear that the work is to some extent designed to be read as an exciting and stirring story that reaches its dramatic peak in its description of the life and death of King Arthur. Geoffrey drew on a number of sources including the work of the 9th century monk Nennius, and an unnamed but extremely ancient Welsh work which he mentions several times. It is clear that he was also drawing on the long Celtic tradition of oral storytelling represented by the Mabinogion. Geoffrey himself is thought to have been of either Welsh or Breton origin and so would have been familiar with these tales.

His history begins in 12 BC with the arrival in the British Isles of Brutus, the great-grandson of Aeneas of Troy. He credits him with naming the country after himself and colonising it and goes on to trace Arthur's ancestry back to the mythical figure of Brutus. Geoffrey is generally considered the first author to elevate Arthur from the role of a powerful military leader or chieftain to a king. It is thought that much of what Geoffrey wrote was informed by a strong political agenda. At the close of his account, in the reign of Cadwallader, the British have been divided into two groups under the pressure of the invading pagan Saxons. Those who have remained in Britain and who are now called the Welsh have retreated to the far west of Britain whilst the other group have fled to what is now Brittany and Northern France. (The term Welsh is itself derived from the Saxon word for foreigner.) Geoffrey can be seen as justifying the Norman invasion of Britain and suggesting that the British and the Normans share a common past and a common enemy in the Saxons.

This would have pleased the Norman kings but Geoffrey's book remains a work of British patriotism as well, one that creates a vivid and impressive history for the Britons, full of heroism and military success. The Celtic roots of the Arthurian tradition are not forgotten as the figure of Merlin takes a place of great importance in the narrative. His prophecies are a great focus of the book, demonstrating Geoffrey's dramatic flair and talent for embellishment and pleasing his audience.

Wace

A Norman writer called Wace, thought to have been a poet and cleric, used *The History of the Kings of Britain* for his work *Roman de Brut* in 1155. The story of the 'Romance of Brutus', written not in Latin but in the vernacular language of the period, was the first of the French Romances. It was dedicated to Eleanor of Aquitaine who was the wife of Henry II. Again there appears to have been political motivation in its commission by Henry who wanted to show the Norman kings to be the descendants of King Arthur and therefore the returning and rightful rulers of Britain.

Wace's poetic tale combined the 'factual' material of Geoffrey's work with romantic and chivalrous elements. Importantly Wace introduces a twelve-year period of peace between Arthur's defeat of the Saxons and his later battles in Europe. This allows a continuation of the adventures and fantasies that appear in the Celtic sources and, in later works, creates the necessary space for the Grail quest to take place. Wace was the first writer to introduce the concept of the Round Table.

Chrétien de Troyes

In the work of the French medieval romance writer Chrétien de Troyes we find the first surviving literary reference to the Grail or Graal. At this point the Grail appears in a Christian context but is not yet specifically described as the cup of the Last Supper. His story *Conte del Graal*, 'story of the Grail', also known as *Perceval*, combines the popular Celtic folk stories of King Arthur with the concepts of the chivalric knight and courtly love. Chrétien can be credited with making a number of innovations in the Arthurian tradition and a number of key ideas are traced to his work. His romances introduce the figure of Lancelot du Lac, a new addition at this time who was not present in the first Celtic tales.

The love triangle of Arthur, Lancelot and Guinevere is a theme that becomes central to many later versions of the story and is based mainly on Chrétien's narratives. But perhaps most importantly, certainly in this context, he is the first to use the term 'Graal', interpreted as meaning Grail.

Very little is actually known about Chrétien and there has been much debate about the date at which his stories first appeared but it is thought that most of his work was produced between 1170 and 1190. He was attached to the courts of Eleanor of Aquitaine and her daughter, Marie de Champagne. The romances that he wrote reflected changes and developments that were happening in Europe, and specifically France, at this time, not least of which was the growing concept of leisure. His stories were written, in part at least, as entertainment for his powerful female patrons and incorporated ideas about the nature of love that were popular in this period.

The Norman conquest of Britain in 1066 had important repercussions for the growth and spread of stories and literature. One of the consequences of the meeting of different cultures through war is often, if unexpectedly, the transference of ideas and beliefs from one group of people to another. In this instance the Celtic tales of King Arthur were to find their way through bards and storytellers into the royal courts of Brittany and Northern France.

The earliest Celtic stories, as typified by the Mabinogion, contain much symbolism and metaphor in their more fantastical details but Chrétien further develops the psychological complexity of his Arthurian tales. The struggles and difficulties undertaken by the later quest knights can be read as inner journeys in which they seek to confront unknown dangers and, in doing so, ultimately confront themselves. In this sense his work can be seen as exploratory and intentionally instructional. Arthur himself is often located as an important yet peripheral figure in these stories. His court becomes the starting point for the challenges of individual knights such as Perceval and Gawain. He is a measure of status and power but he has a regal role rather than an active participatory one. This forms a major difference between the early Celtic tales and the later French romances.

Chivalry

The heroism of the protagonists of the Celtic stories survives into the French interpretations but is developed and combined with the chivalric ideal. The origin of the word chivalry can be traced to the French word for horseman, *chevalier*. In chivalry a number of elements combined to form a code of behaviour and honour for the knights of the Middle Ages. Battle prowess was still an important facet of the knight's role but this was tempered by a commitment to Christian ideals and the protection and assistance of women. Chivalry demanded high standards of fairness, self-control, loyalty and a commitment to justice and mercy. The influence of a new courtly sophistication of manner and deportment becomes intertwined with courageous actions in the romances of Chrétien de Troyes. Whether or not real knights of the Middle Ages achieved such lofty ideals is debatable but certainly the training and ritual for being knighted was extremely religious and involved meditation and self-reflection. After first serving his apprenticeship as a page and later an esquire the initiate would become a knight. Significantly he would be required to hold a night-long vigil in a chapel before taking Holy Communion and finally being dubbed a knight. It was an honour normally restricted to the aristocracy. As landowners and important figures in society they had a duty to uphold justice and the law of the king.

Although Chrétien de Troyes does not make the Grail a specifically Christian artefact he does set it in a Christian context that later writers would underline. The importance of Holy Communion would become reflected in the Christian image of the Grail, the most holy of cups. The romances offer us a mirror in which the society that created them becomes reflected.

Chrétien de Troyes died before finishing *Conte del Graal* but the popularity of his story was such that several attempts were made to complete it. The enigmatic nature of the Grail in Chrétien's story left its origins unexplored and added to its already considerable air of mystery. At its close Perceval has failed to heal the Fisher King and the wasteland by remaining silent when he witnesses the Grail procession. A hermit informs him that he should have asked the purpose of the Grail and the meaning of the procession.

There is some inference in the tale that, had it been completed, Perceval would have gone on to achieve the Grail quest and by asking the ritual question so healed the Fisher King, ended his suffering and restored his rule to the kingdom. However, this is conjecture and the tale leaves many questions unresolved and unanswered.

The concept of the Grail adds a spiritual, Christian dimension to Arthur's knights that is intended to reflect medieval ideals about the conduct, behaviour and beliefs of the perfect knight. It was expected of all knights at this time that they would participate in the holy crusades so the image of the questing Christian soldier had solid roots in the real lives of medieval people.

Courtly Love

The concept of courtly love became an important influence on the Arthurian tales, particularly in the work of Chrétien de Troyes. Like chivalry it was an ideal that developed in the upper echelons of European society around the time of the crusades. Essentially romantic love was raised to an almost religious level of intensity and meaning. Courtly love by its very nature had an adulterous aspect to it. A woman who was the focus of courtly love was exalted and revered and she became the object of complete adoration by her lover. Lancelot reveres Guinevere in this way but knows that she is the wife and Queen of King Arthur and is tortured by this. Chrétien de Troyes seems to have drawn some of his ideas from the Roman poet Ovid who suggested that love should be governed by a code of conduct in which the admirer should give everything to the object of his affections.

Troubadours

During the 12th and 13th centuries the Languedoc area of Southern France produced a new style of musical poetic expression that focused on the great themes of courtly love and romance. This artistic movement is especially associated with minstrels of the region known as the troubadors.

Robert de Boron

After the work of Chrétien de Troyes the most significant development in the literature relating to the Grail is its explicit Christianisation by Robert de Boron. In his stories the Grail specifically becomes the cup of Joseph of Arimathea which Christ himself used at the Last Supper and in which Joseph caught Christ's blood. Once again attempts at dating these works have proved controversial, but they are generally thought to have been written in the period 1200–1210. They include *L'Estoire du Graal* (*Romance of the History of the Grail*), *Joseph of Arimathea, Merlin* and *Perceval*. Where Chrétien de Troyes had introduced the idea of the Grail into the context of the Arthurian tales, Robert de Boron makes the Grail the focus of the narrative. He relates the story of Arthur's life but starts and finishes his prose cycle with the story and significance of the Grail.

Much of the material found in his version of the Grail history is drawn from what are known as the Apocrypha or apocryphal gospels. Essentially, these were Christian texts that were left out of the Bible when it was finalised as a whole in the 2nd century AD. Before this event there had been a whole body of work in existence that related to the Old and New Testaments. Although rejected from inclusion in this version of the Bible, many works survived and some of the Old Testament stories were included in the Apocrypha of the English King James Bible. The material related to the New Testament, although officially abandoned, did not disappear and became very popular when translated from Greek and Latin sources into 'everyday' languages such as English, French and German. Versions of these texts translated into verse in France in the 12th century were also well known.

Previously much religious literature had only been available to the Latin-reading priests and clergy and most people were unable to read it. With an increasingly literate population with a taste for Christian literature these tales flourished. Robert de Boron successfully combined these religious sources with the popular stories of the chivalry and adventures of King Arthur's Knights. By merging these elements Robert de Boron also succeeded in giving his work an air of authority and credibility that affects his narrative style. It is recounted as a history and, rooted in Christian texts, strives for a new level of authenticity. However, as we have seen, this is not the first time fact and fiction has been blended in the story of the Grail.

The *Vulgate Cycle*

It is thought that a group of Cistercian monks produced the large and comprehensive epic known as the *Vulgate Cycle*, which is also referred to as the *Prose Lancelot.* An anonymous work, it was produced roughly between 1210 and 1240 and relates the histories of the Grail and King Arthur in considerable depth. Beginning with the origins of the Grail itself, as related to the lives of Jesus Christ and Joseph of Arimathea, it chooses as its central focus the figure of Lancelot who was introduced to Arthur's court by Chrétien de Troyes. The *Vulgate Cycle* ends with the deaths of Lancelot, Arthur and Guinevere.

The emphasis is on establishing the noble heritage and background of Lancelot as the best knight in the world.

In this story Lancelot is deceived by the effects of a magical drink into thinking that Helaine, the Grail maiden, is his true love Guinevere. They sleep together and she becomes pregnant. The result of the deception is that Helaine gives birth to Galahad who is destined to achieve the Grail and free her father's realm from a curse that has made it into a wasteland. However so intense is the experience of Galahad when he looks into the Grail that he dies in a vision of spiritual ecstasy and the Grail and the lance of the legionary Longinus, which is the spear that pierced the side of Christ on the cross, are taken up to heaven by a disembodied hand.

Parzival

Of all the different versions of the Grail story, perhaps the most unusual and individual interpretation is that provided by the German poet Wolfram von Eschenbach. Written between 1210 and 1220, his romance *Parzival* offers the greatest representational departure in its depiction of the form that the Grail takes. In previous descriptions it has been described sometimes as a shallow dish but mainly as a cup, goblet, chalice or bowl. Eschenbach sets his Grail castle at Munsalvaesche, which probably means Mount Salvation, where the company of the wounded King is fed by the miracle of the Grail in the form of a stone. The Grail in stone form can provide nourishment with limitless food and drink and creates a feast that Parzival partakes of at Munsalvaesche. It also has the power to bestow youthfulness and prolong life on those who see it. There is a suggestion that it can bring physical resurrection as it is described as having had the power to restore the Phoenix back to life after it has been burnt to ashes. There are many Eastern influences in Eschenbach's work and some have interpreted his Grail stone as representing the Philosopher's Stone. The search for this magical stone became a great quest in itself for medieval alchemists who believed that it could be combined with base metals to produce gold. The alchemists were engaged in what they called the Great Work, which for some had its highest aims in reaching spiritual perfection and union with God. In this sense the stone is an important catalytic element and intermediary between earth and heaven, a role that finds echoes, of course, in the concept of the Grail.

The main focus of Eschenbach's tale is the noble lineage and story of the title character and the fulfilment of his individual destiny. Parzival's father Gahmuret experiences exotic and exciting adventures, travelling to Babylon where he has an affair with the heathen Queen Belacane of Zazamanc. Gahmuret leaves her to return to the West where he marries and fathers Parzival. However, he returns to the East to help an old friend, the Baruc of Baghdad, and is killed fighting the Babylonians. The source and inspiration for much of this material would, of course, have been the crusades. Amidst the violence and conflict of the wars between crusaders and Saracens cultural exchanges took place and this is reflected in Eschenbach's story.

Malory

Of all those people who told and re-told the Arthurian epics in the Middle Ages, perhaps no single writer did more to produce an all-encompassing version of the stories than Thomas Malory. His version, although heavily edited by the publisher William Caxton, became for many, including the writers and poets of the 18th and 19th centuries, the definitive account of the life and death of King Arthur and the associated Grail quest.

Malory appears to have been extremely familiar with the litera-ture on this subject but drew particularly heavily from the *Vulgate Cycle*. He is credited with transforming the material into a heightened, dramatic, action-filled adventure. The achievements and heroism of Arthur's knights are set in a romantic and chivalrous context. This sits in stark counter-point to the circumstances of Malory's own life when he was composing what was at first a collection of Arthurian stories. He was a convicted criminal serving time in Newgate Jail in London, who had in the course of his lifetime been accused of a variety of crimes. He had been tried variously for murder, rape, robbery, extortion and the theft of cattle. Malory was imprisoned on eight occasions for periods of time that varied from several days to two and a half years. On two occasions he escaped confinement, on the first swimming the moat at Coleshill prison on the 27 July 1451 and on the second fighting his way out of Colchester Jail in October 1454.

He wrote a series of books whilst confined in Newgate Jail that he completed in 1470. They were collected together and edited by William Caxton under the overall title of *Le Morte d'Arthur* in 1485. It was Caxton that unified the books that Malory had written, creating one whole coherent story from the original material.

3

GLASTONBURY AND THE GRAIL

Glastonbury

Glastonbury plays a particularly strong and resonant role in the Grail tradition. Most obviously it is the place that Joseph of Arimathea is said to have brought the Grail and, it is claimed, founded the first Christian church in Europe. As an actual physical location it offers an excellent example of the way in which the symbolism and nature of the Grail can be seen to evolve. Underlying its fame and status as a centre for Christian worship and its association with Joseph of Arimathea is a landscape and a location with an extremely ancient and pagan past.

The geology and topography of Glastonbury Tor have exerted a powerful influence over people from the earliest of times. Its unusual and sometimes surprising properties have provoked both awe and wonder and its symbolism has been assimilated and incorporated into very nearly every belief system that has encountered and interpreted it. Located approximately fifteen miles from the sea, the town of Glastonbury today is situated in the southwest of Britain in Somerset. The low flat nature of the surrounding countryside is reflected in the term 'Somerset levels'. The fertile farming areas of the Somerset levels were for many thousands of years marsh land that were often prone to flooding. Glastonbury is located in the eastern part of the levels. At one point following the last Ice Age the area was in fact a shallow inland sea.

Glastonbury itself is situated in an area of higher ground that forms an island rising above the surrounding locality. During its long history of inundations it gained the name of the Isle of Avalon. It has also been referred to as Ynis Witrin or the 'Isle of Glass'. During pre-history it is thought that people would have fished in the shallow waters nearby or hunted for duck. Jutting out of the mists of the marsh the island would have been a visually striking landscape feature and its naming as the Isle of Glass may have derived from the waters that surrounded it. In Celtic mythology many tales focus on islands supposedly made of glass, such as Bardsey Island off the Lleyn Peninsular in North Wales. Similarly, recurrent references to revolving castles reached by Grail questers perhaps have their basis in islands reached by boat. Bardsey Island is infamous for its strong and treacherous tides that make sailing around it difficult. This combined with visual phenomena such as mist, cloud and the reflection of sunlight gives a plausible and comprehensible basis for these magical descriptions.

Glastonbury is also remarkable for the two springs that flow from a valley between the base of the Tor and Chalice Hill. They are located approximately fifty metres apart but are very different in their mineral content and appearance. The White Spring has a high content of calcium carbonate and it is thought it originally flowed out of a cave with distinctive mineral formations that has subsequently been sealed over. The second spring rises at Chalice Well and has a high iron content giving it a distinctive red colour that creates a rusty residual deposit. This spring is sometimes referred to as the 'Blood Spring'.

An earthwork in the form of a ditch, which cuts through the causeway that connects the island created by the Tor to the nearest high ground amplifies and completes the appearance of it being a separate body of land. It is thought to have been

created during the Iron Age and that it was intended to deline-
ate a 'sacred space' rather than to be used for defensive or
settlement purposes.

The placement of the Tor in the west of Britain in the
direction of the setting sun, in conjunction with its distinctive
springs and connected subterranean cave systems, make this
a compelling site for mystical symbolism. Glastonbury Tor
has been shaped into a rising spiral of terraces running from
its broad base to the summit where the church tower built in
the 14th century now stands. The terraces were farmed and
developed during the medieval period by the monks of
Glastonbury but, although estimates vary, it has been
suggested that their original creation may date back to the
Neolithic period. They may have served a ritual purpose
rather than a practical one.

The Tor springs correspond with Celtic descriptions of a
cavernous gateway to the Underworld and it is likely that the
Tor has been a focus for ritual cult belief for thousands of
years.

The gushing springs and their vivid colours have become
connected symbolically with the sweat and blood of Christ
but it seems likely that they were preceded by a Celtic and a
pre-Celtic belief system.The Tor itself can be seen as a recumbent landscape goddess with the springs being representative
of fertility and the perpetual cycle of life and death. As with
many other sacred sites around the world Glastonbury
became an important focus for Christianity. From approximately the 7th century AD onward Glastonbury was the site
of Christian worship that culminated in the building of the
medieval abbey.

In Geoffrey of Monmouth's *History of the Kings of Britain*
King Arthur is fatally wounded and borne away to the
mysterious Isle of Avalon to be healed. A constant feature of
the Arthurian tales is that the King does not die but will
return when he is needed most by Britain. Often the Isle of
Avalon, ruled over by the enchantress Morgan Le Fay, is the

place where he is taken but in some versions he lies sleeping in a cave surrounded by his knights. During the late 12th century the monks of Glastonbury 'discovered' the grave of Arthur and Guinevere in the grounds of the Abbey. This helped boost the profile and earning capacity of the Abbey as a place of pilgrimage. This increase in revenue and prestige raises doubts about the authenticity of the discovery. It also greatly benefited the monarchy in that it put an end to any suggestion that Arthur would return to overthrow the Norman rulers.

The sanctity and importance of Glastonbury is most importantly developed in the story of the arrival of Joseph of Arimathea who buried the Holy Grail at the foot of Chalice Hill. It is said that the waters rising from the Chalice spring were turned red by the blood of Christ. Where the Tor may once have been representative of the Neolithic Earth Goddess and later the Iron Age Goddess with her attendant cauldron and its life-giving properties, Christianity transformed the hill into a calvary mount linked through the Grail and the red spring with the body and resurrection of Christ.

Joseph of Arimathea

As we have already seen Joseph of Arimathea plays a key role in the medieval Grail stories and, other than Christ, he is the Biblical character most closely associated with it. However, like the Grail itself, there remains something mysterious and elusive about his identity and his relationship to the chalice cup. In the Bible Joseph is said to be part of a group known as the Sanhedrin who governed Jerusalem during the Roman occupation. Joseph is a wealthy Jewish leader with some political influence who obtains the body of Christ following the crucifixion. In various accounts Joseph gains the cup which was used by Christ at the Last Supper and catches some blood which flows from the wound in his side made by the lance of the Roman soldier Longinus. In some versions he collects this blood whilst Christ is on the cross, in others whilst his body is being prepared for burial. Robert de Boron appears to have drawn heavily on the apocryphal Gospel of Nicodemus for the material contained in his *Joseph of Arimathea*, which was written around 1190. In this version Joseph is imprisoned by the Jews following the disappearance of Christ's body from the tomb. He is denied food as punishment for the robbery of the body.

During his imprisonment the resurrected Christ appears in his cell and gives the cup to Joseph. He also shares secret teachings including instruction in the mystery of the Mass. He vanishes, but Joseph is kept alive by the daily appearance of a dove that places a wafer in the cup. Upon his release in AD70 he departs from the Holy Land to spread the word of Jesus.

Most medieval Grail romances have Joseph bringing the cup to Western Europe, stopping in some accounts first in France and then travelling on to Britain to found the first church at Glastonbury. In Robert de Boron's *Le Roman du Graal* Joseph hands the Grail to the Fisher King, Brons. It is then Brons who brings the Grail to Britain. In his book *The Head of God* Keith Laidler argues that, 'There is much evidence to indicate that the two Grail characters, Joseph of Arimathea and the Fisher King, are in fact, one and the same individual'. (Keith Laidler, *The Head of God*, p157.)

Throughout the medieval Grail romances the idea that Perceval, Lancelot or his son Galahad are in some way related either to the Fisher King or Joseph of Arimathea recurs. In the Mabinogion tale *Peredur* and in the French *Le Conte du Graal* and *Perlesvaus* a macabre reference is made to a severed head, which is named as being Perceval's cousin. In the *Peredur* it is carried on a dish in a procession together with a spear that drips blood. Laidler hypothesises that the object of veneration and importance in these tales is not the Grail as holy vessel but the severed head. Essentially, he links the lineage of the Grail knights to Joseph of Arimathea and argues that Joseph himself is related to Christ. This unorthodox view is an attempt to explain some of the more bizarre and disjointed elements of

these tales. Laidler views the tales as encoded heretical allego-
ries that relate to an ancient worship of severed heads and that
the recurrent image in the romances of a severed head is a
reference to this and, more specifically, represents the head of
Jesus.

Certainly there seems to be an attempt to establish a lineage
of Grail kings reaching back logically to Joseph of Arimathea
and Christ himself. As we have seen the material upon which
much of the Grail romances were based is drawn from the
Apocryphal Gospels and other Christian sources rejected from
the Bible.

The suggestion that the Grail romances allude to a divergent
strand of Christianity is not as unlikely as it may first appear.
At this time in medieval history the Roman Catholic Church
was engaged in a process of standardising Christian teachings
along a patriarchal model and in many ways was diverging
from the early teachings of the Church, as for example in the
case of the re-interpreted Eucharist.

The terrible inquisitions that were carried out in Europe
during this period focused on Christian groups such as the
Cathars who refused to conform to Catholicism. This was very
much a period of change for Christianity and much that had
been tolerated previously became heretical and taboo.

The stories of Joseph's arrival at Glastonbury have other
variants in which he reaches Britain with his small company
carrying two cruets, one of gold and another of silver. They
were said to contain the blood and sweat of Christ and again to
have issued from his wounds on the cross. These two elements,
of course, match the white and red springs and create a successful allegory for the coming of Christianity to Britain. This is
matched by the story that Joseph and his exhausted group
arrived at Glastonbury in December at a site now called
Wearyall Hill. He planted his staff in the ground and, miraculously, it blossomed. Interestingly, the thorn that grows on this
hill and blossoms at Christmas originates from the Middle
East.

Chalice Well

Rising from the foot of Chalice Hill at Glastonbury the red spring with its high iron content is best known today as Chalice Well. The strong Christian connotations of the spring are borne out by its current name although this is, in fact, very recent, dating only from the last century. (In the 18th century and earlier it was referred to as St Joseph's Well.) The term Blood Spring is of a similar age. Much earlier documents refer to it as 'Chalcwell' (AD 1256), although there is some confusion as to whether this actually refers to the White Spring instead. (For the majority of their history the two springs ran freely and indeed would have met and flowed together. They are now separated by re-channelling.)

It appears that the grove of yew trees in which Chalice Well is set is of an extremely ancient provenance. An archaeological excavation found buried yew stumps that dated from the Roman occupation. Evidence was found that the site had also been used in pre-history. The symbolism of the blood of Christ caught in the Grail cup and the resurrection of the soul through his suffering and death find obvious echoes in the Blood Spring. But it is likely that the site of Chalice Well would have been the scene of pre-Christian worship also. For the Celts the yew tree was a symbol of death and rebirth and to find these trees persistently and constantly present at such a site suggests a long-held fascination with its unusual appearance.

Most obviously the spring emerges from the rocks beneath the Tor and would probably have been regarded as an entrance to the Underworld by both Celtic and pre-Celtic peoples. Because the springs are now built upon and channelled it is difficult to know exactly how they would have appeared. However, commentators writing in the 19th century, before the White Spring was covered by a reservoir, describe the spring emerging from a cavern or grotto and coating everything it touched with a surface of white calcium.

A common theme, associated with the Chalice Well even

today and likely to be of ancient origin, is that of healing. Certainly springs and wells are traditionally sites that people have visited in every known era to cure illnesses and at nearby Bath the Celtic cult of the goddess Sulis was particularly well known. In the Roman era the Goddess is referred to as Sulis-Minerva, Minerva being the Roman equivalent, but Sulis remains the most important deity. The hot water that flows from the springs by the river Avon was channelled and enclosed by Roman engineers and would previously have been worshipped in its natural state.

Wookey Hole, a spectacular cavern close to Glastonbury, also has links with goddess worship or, at least, acknowledgement of her power and can be seen as representing an Underworld ruled by a female deity. She is known tellingly as the 'Wise Woman' or, in a description that reflects Christian prejudice, as the 'Witch of Wookey Hole'.

The legend of Joseph of Arimathea burying the cruets containing the sweat and blood of Jesus, and more famously the Holy Grail, at the source of the Red Spring itself has strong echoes of pre-Christian ritual. As we saw in Chapter One, Celtic peoples made many votive offerings at aquatic sites such as lakes, rivers, springs and sometimes wells. The deposition of cauldrons at such sites, with their connotations of regeneration, fertility and plenty, echo the magical powers of the Grail. Darker themes of ritual death may also be represented in this context as the cauldron was also used for sacrificial purposes. A moulding on a plate of the Gunderstrup cauldron of a god-figure holding a man over a vessel may reflect this and it has been suggested blood offerings were caught in ceremonial vessels by the Celts. But the Celts also believed in re-birth through reincarnation and the ritual death of Jesus can, in some senses, be seen as echoing this tradition. Such vessels, like the Grail, can symbolically encompass both life and death and, in the setting of the Red Spring, become particularly evocative. The life-giving waters of the goddess become the blood of Christ flowing through a seemingly preserved ritual grove of yew trees with its connotations of both death and re-birth and, in a Christian setting, protection from evil spirits.

Yew trees, of course, are found in Christian graveyards across Europe and were sometimes planted on parish boundaries to ward off evil spirits. Their red berries have toxic qualities linked to death but their evergreen nature has strong associations with renewal and vigour. However, the powerful symbolism of the springs rising and flowing across the landscape is intensified and made even more compelling by the source from which it emerges, the subterranean Underworld.

Underworld

In the Celtic tale *Preiddeu Annwn*, found in the Mabinogion, Arthur and a company of heroes lead a raid into the Underworld known as Annwn in search of a magic cauldron. Annwn is not necessarily comparable to the Christian concept of Hell and, although it is generally described as an underground realm, it is sometimes portrayed as an island. Annwn is ruled over by the deity king Arawn and the cauldron is said to be housed in a 'revolving' castle. The theme of a dangerous quest linked to a sacred vessel has clear parallels with the questing knights and their search for the Christian Grail. Like the later knights, few return from Annwn because of the dangers that are encountered on their journey.

The descriptions of otherworldly islands in the West, surrounded by water and with entrances to the Underworld, that are found in Celtic mythology have drawn parallels with Glastonbury Tor. Local legend and folklore describe a portal to the Underworld guarded by the mythical figure of Gwynn Ap Nudd, or the 'White Son of Night'. Saint Collen, a Welsh Christian figure of the 7th century, is said to have visited Annwn himself only to cause it to disappear by sprinkling holy water on Glastonbury Tor. Such folkloric tales lend credence to the suggestion that Glastonbury Tor, with its springs and cavernous grottoes, was a site for pagan ceremonies and rituals focused on the concept of a subterranean Underworld. At certain times of the year, most notably Samhain, the pagan festival that corresponds to Halloween, Gwyn Ap Nudd and the Wild Hunt (composed of spectral horses and the Cwm Annwn, the Welsh hell-hounds) were said to search for souls to take into Annwn.

The theme of heroes questing and entering into or contacting the Underworld is one found throughout world cultures and mythologies. In Homer's *The Odyssey* the Greek hero Odysseus travels to the Oracle of the Dead or Necromantion to seek help and advice on how to return to his home on the island of Ithaca and speaks to the shades of his fallen comrades from the Trojan War. Like the Grail quest the journey of Odysseus is long and arduous and requires bravery, resilience and strength. The Gods put many tests in his path. The Underworld, as Homer describes it, is located across the river Styx. Dead souls are ferried across the river by the boatman Charon to the Underworld which is ruled by Hades. The Underworld of Greek mythology is not exactly comparable to Hell in the Christian sense although some stratification of the afterlife is described.

Interestingly the entrance to the Underworld is guarded by the terrifying dog Cerberus which echoes the hounds of Annwn. Dogs appear in Celtic iconography accompanying deities such as Nodens, Diana and Epona. Skeletons of dogs have been found in ritual graves and settings at numerous locations in Britain and Europe. The symbolism and association with death through hunting is often accompanied by representations of dogs having a healing symbolism. As we have seen Glastonbury has traditions that incorporate an Underworld with ghostly canines, a healing tradition of wells and springs and the restorative qualities of the Holy Grail. The presence of all these related mythologies and stories offer clues to, and evidence of, its ancient past.

Scholars and historians put the most likely site for the Oracle of the Dead at a site in the Epirus region of Greece near the river Acheron. The Necromantion is located on a small hill near the coast and would once have been partially surrounded by a great body of water in the form of a lake. A chamber probably caused by water erosion became the central 'Hall of Hades' where pilgrims came to ask advice of the dead. Offerings were made of food, drink and other gifts and placed in large sacred vessels to enlist the help of the deceased. The setting and associated imagery of the site evokes comparisons with Glastonbury as a site of ancient ritual. Pilgrims are thought to have taken hallucinogenic substances in the form of seeds and drinks before achieving their 'visions'. The rituals would last a whole lunar month and would end with several days of purification and restoration. The elements of arduous preparation and journeying, an intense visionary experience and purification find striking echoes in the Grail romances suggesting that these are themes rooted in the most ancient world religions.

The Greeks set their Elysian fields in the West, the region in which the Celts placed their magical isles. The Underworld could not be entered by mortals, except by heroes with great cunning and skill or those who performed brave feats. Heroes such as Orpheus and Heracles and, in Celtic mythology, Arthur.

For many cultures grave goods were extremely important in aiding the deceased in their journey into the Underworld. High status goods often reflected their role in the realms of the living but, just as importantly, food and drink were placed in the burial to sustain them on their difficult journey. In many Celtic burials in Southern England hobnail boots have been discovered with the deceased. There are even examples of the burial of infants being accompanied by adult shoes suggesting a belief that the child would become an adult in the Underworld.

The twin concerns of difficult journeying and the provision of plenty and abundance curiously emerge through the iconography of the Grail, although with the development of Christianity the emphasis moves from Underworld associations to mountain tops and 'sky' settings.

Annwn, like the Elysian fields, is often portrayed as a happy place of feasting and enjoyment unburdened by mortal cares such as old age, illness and want. The cauldron of Annwn provides limitless food and plenty but, like the Christian Grail, has discriminatory qualities. In this instance the cauldron will not provide food for a coward. From the realm of the physical and the sensual the Grail develops as an altogether more transcendent and spiritual symbol. Only the purest knight such as Galahad can achieve the quest for the Grail and he dies almost immediately, illustrating Christian beliefs that real fulfilment and happiness can only occur in an ethereal heaven and not in the earthly world of original sin.

However, later Christian versions of Grail myths share and retain a number of the Celtic mythical elements, not least in their depiction of the Wasteland restored through the achievement of the quest. The fertility of the land, which is linked to the injured Fisher King, can only be restored through the asking of the ritual question. Usually this question is, 'Who does the Grail serve?' The answer is normally, 'The Fisher King' and, by extension, the land.

In some versions the Grail is said to have the power to make the trees flower. As a symbol of life, bridging the Underworld and the sky through roots and branches, the tree has an extremely ancient symbolism in world cultures. In Norse mythology Yggdrasil is the great world tree, an ash that binds the cosmos together. With three roots that pass into the Underworld of Niflheim, Jotunheim, the home of the giants, and Asgard, where the Gods live, it is a central focus for all things. At Glastonbury Tor the traditions of pagan cultures reflected in the image of the world tree can be seen to take on Christian form in the myth of the flowering of the Holy Thorn associated with Joseph of Arimathea.

4

ARTHUR AND THE HOLY GRAIL

King Arthur

A number of ironies surround the mysterious and iconic legend of King Arthur. One is that a figure that has become so steeped in a tradition of fantasy and imagination may actually have existed. There is real documentary and archaeological evidence to suggest that an Arthur or someone very like him was alive in Britain during the 5th century AD and successfully united and defended Britain from successive waves of incomers such as the Saxons, Angles and Jutes. He may actually be a composite of several leaders whose achievements have been heightened and combined by bards, writers and historians but there remains substance amongst the extraordinary tales relating to his life and exploits. It is also remarkable that Arthur has come to be universally regarded as an English king. In truth, he was almost certainly a Welsh leader who, after the Celtic Britons had been effectively driven westwards, fought off the Angles or English at a time before 'Angle-land' or England was established.

The name of Arthur was a yardstick for bravery and military success from around the 5th century AD onwards and in many early Welsh accounts he is not specifically described as a king. It may be more realistic to view him as an effective war chieftain who, for a short period, succeeded in uniting the disparate groups and chiefdoms of Britain following the withdrawal of the Roman legions from Britain. The decline of the Roman Empire and its relinquishment of its former provinces left Britain particularly vulnerable to attack from European tribal raiders. This period of semi-chaos and division is the most likely period in which a real Arthur would have existed.

During the Roman occupation Christianity had been brought to Britain and, towards the end of that period, deals were brokered with some small groups of Saxons so that they could hold lands in Britain in return for helping protect against and fight any other incomers. Writers such as Geoffrey of Monmouth describe the British as being ruled by a King Vortigern in the first part of the 5th century AD who continues this process of deal-making with settlers but is finally betrayed when they renege on their promises and conflict and violence break out. Once again there appears to be a factual basis in this story as the name Vortigern refers simply to the most prominent leader or ruler amongst a group of kings or chieftains. In the wake of these events a leader called Ambrosius Aurelianus galvanised the British and fought back against the Saxons. A measure of success was achieved and a number of the Iron Age hill-forts that had been deserted during the Roman period were reoccupied and turned into military strongholds.

Written records of the later part of the 6th century show that a man named Arthur had become widely celebrated at this time as a British military leader suggesting that Ambrosius Aurelianus could have served under his rule. It is this real period of British history when, if only for a few decades, this invasion was contained that the legend of King Arthur emerges. The great themes of the Arthurian traditions appear to have their roots in this time when the British have restored some control over the country and have a degree of unity. The embellishments of the bards celebrate this victory in stories that blended Celtic myth and reality.

A monk called Nennius writing in the 9th century provides probably the first reference to a King Arthur in a historical account in his *Historia Brittonum* (*History of the Britons*). His account gives Arthur as the chief leader in the fight against hordes of incoming Saxons that reaches its climax at the bloody Battle of Mount Badon. Arthur is also described as being a Christian in Nennius' account. However, this and other similar written records can not be regarded as entirely reliable.

What is indisputable is that Arthur became widely known and celebrated in the Middle Ages and that his popularity has continued up to the present day. He is a unique figure in history and mythology whose legend can be seen to have contributed greatly to the development of Western literature and art. It was this fame and popularity that led the writers of the medieval romances to attach the story of the Grail to his reign. Many writers have observed that the story of the Grail sits somewhat uneasily in the canon of Arthurian legend and it could be argued that it becomes a major factor in the weakening and final break-up of Arthur's mythical golden age. Many knights set out in search of the Grail and, pursuing a goal that is doomed to be fruitless, many never return. Although some knights come close to the Grail in that they find its location and have strange experiences and adventures on their journeys, it is only the chosen few (in most stories, it is only Galahad, who was born to achieve the quest) who finally undergo a mystical and ultimately fatal communion with God.

Merlin and the Grail Quest

The popular conception of Merlin derives mainly from the work of Geoffrey of Monmouth. Merlin is a fascinating character who towers over the Arthurian myths and, in many ways, is the creator of, and catalyst for, its major themes. As with King Arthur it is likely that real historical figures went into his literary creation but, above and beyond the historical reality, lie the ancient Celtic traditions that he embodies and symbolises.

The most obvious source for the imagery attached to the character of Merlin is the important Celtic religious caste known as the Druids. The Celts had three orders or castes of priests – the Bards, the Ovates and the Druids. Powerful advisors and decision-makers, the Druids not only had an important secular function, often acting as judges or officiators in cases of disagreements or law breaking, but they also acted as a link between the mortal world and the realm of the gods and goddesses. Divination and prophecy were major aspects of their roles and it is fitting that a figure such as Merlin should appear within the Arthurian tradition.

It seems that Geoffrey based his character on at least two people recorded in Welsh and Scottish histories. These he combined with other material to create the great wizard and seer. In medieval Scottish literature there are stories of an important noble called Lailoken who is advisor to King Gwenddoleu and is driven mad following a battle at Arfderydd, Cumbria, in which his patron is killed and his forces largely destroyed. King Gwenddoleu was a pagan ruler who fought the Christian king, Rhydderch – in all likelihood in a dispute over land. During the battle Merlin/Lailoken is said to hear a voice that accuses him of being responsible for the slaughter and claims that he will be punished for it. He flees into the forests to live a simple, poor life, close to the natural world, with only animals and birds for company. During a period of fifty years of living in the wilderness he gains the gift of second sight and is able to foretell the future. The Welsh called him 'Myrddin Wylt' or Wild Merlin, setting his story in the 6th century AD. His name is said to indicate a connection with the town of Camarthen in South Wales. There are suggestions of a shamanic role in his life in the forest communicating with animals and the spirit world.

Another source for the character of Merlin is a Welsh legend set in the 5th century AD and first recorded by Nennius. It concerns a strange boy, born without a human father, who Geoffrey of Monmouth later suggests is conceived through supernatural means. He is born with the gift of second sight and is able to predict future events. He becomes an advisor to King Vortigern. The boy, called Ambrosius, plays an important role in divining the future of Britain. King Vortigern attempts to build a tower or fortress at Dina Emrys in Snowdonia, where he has fled following his betrayal by the Saxons, but the tower keeps collapsing. Ambrosius reveals that the foundations are built on a hollow stone that contains two fighting dragons. It is the fighting of the dragons that is destroying attempts to build on the site. The red and white dragons are said to symbolise the warring English and Welsh or British and Saxons.

In the *History of the Kings of Britain* Geoffrey has Merlin not only foretell the coming of Arthur but also engineer the circumstances of his conception. He casts a spell so that King Uther Pendragon is mistaken by the Cornish Queen Igraine, or Ygerna, for her husband Gorlois. Uther visits her at Tintagel Castle and, under the influence of Merlin's spell, she sleeps with him and becomes pregnant with Arthur. Merlin is also said by Geoffrey to be responsible for bringing the massive stones of Stonehenge to England, transporting them from their original home in Ireland. Far-fetched as this description may sound, this again strikes a chord with reality. Modern archaeology has revealed that the stones were originally quarried in distant South Wales before being transported to Wiltshire.

In Robert de Boron's romance Merlin becomes the prophet of the coming of the Grail. It is Merlin who instructs Arthur's father, Uther Pendragon to create the order of the Round Table. Merlin later tells Arthur, when he becomes King, that his destiny is bound up with the Round Table because it will be one of his knights who achieves the quest to heal the Fisher King and become guardian of the Grail which contains the blood of Christ. According to this account, Arthur himself is destined to become Emperor of Rome. Merlin seems to be aware that these events will bring an end to the era of magic or paganism, which he himself represents. In this context Merlin is a character that, in some ways, seems to contradict his own role as a supposedly pagan wizard. However, Robert de Boron solves this problem with an ingenious early plot device. In de Boron's account Merlin's mother is made pregnant by a demon whilst she is sleeping and this is how he gains his supernatural gifts, especially the gift of prophecy. His horrified mother tells her priest who blesses the child and sprinkles holy water on her. Merlin is therefore able to retain his supernatural abilities but uses them for good.

The fellowship of the Round Table will become bound up with the quest for the Holy Grail and the shape of the table is said to echo that of the table of the Last Supper. One seat is left empty and often referred to in Grail literature as the 'Siege Perilous' because it will swallow up any person who is not pure enough to sit there. It is intended for the Grail champion who, in Robert de Boron's version, is Perceval. Just as in Chrétien de Troyes's account Perceval fails to ask the ritual question at the castle of the Fisher King. As a consequence he wanders alone for seven years. It is Merlin in disguise who later intercepts Perceval, who has been jousting in a tournament, and reprimands him for not fulfilling his vow to return to the castle of the Fisher King. He also prophesies that it will take him a year to return there. Perceval does reach the castle, eventually asks the ritual question and the Fisher King is healed. Perceval becomes the keeper of the Grail and is instructed in its mysteries by the departing Fisher King, Brons.

Following these events Arthur marches on France but is betrayed by his nephew Mordred who claims the throne of Britain in his absence. Returning to fight his treacherous nephew, Arthur succeeds in killing him but is himself mortally wounded and carried away to Avalon. Merlin is then described as returning to the Grail castle where Perceval is now king and relating the story of Arthur to the company of the Grail. Fascinatingly, Merlin is then said to retreat to his home outside the Grail castle which he calls his 'esplumoir'. An esplumoir is a cage used to catch the feathers of hawks or birds of prey when they are moulting. It is suggestive of transformative, regenerative change and has underlying implications of the tradition of shamanic shape-shifting and the shaman's ability to change their appearance into an animal or bird.

The Sword in the Stone

An extraordinary image, the sword set in the stone was the contrivance of Merlin to prove Arthur's lineage from King Uther Pendragon. Only the trueborn King was said to be able to draw the sword from the stone and this has become a central symbol in the Arthurian myths. This sword is not generally conceived of as Excalibur and the image of the sword in the stone seems to be a later addition to the legend. Malory, in particular, develops the theme, setting the sword in an anvil on top of a great block of stone with lettering about its base declaring that only the rightful successor to the throne would be able to draw the weapon from its setting. This is an intriguing combination of images. The magnificent sword traditionally represents a warrior elite and the sacred stone in Celtic legend often has links to the revelation of true kingship. In Ireland the Stone of Destiny was the crowning stone that was said to cry out when the true King stood upon it. This stone was carried to Scotland where it was placed in Scone Abbey close to Perth. The Stone of Scone became the crowning stone for the Scottish Kings until it was seized by Edward I of England in 1296. The fact that the terrible and ruthless King Edward should choose to take the Stone of Scone indicates the powerful symbolism that this object possessed. Many other myths have become attached to stones and the theme of rulership and authority. London Stone, which is currently to be found opposite Cannon Street railway station, has a body of myth and history attached to it that portray it as a symbol of power and sovereignty and also attributes it with protective powers over the city.

Over time the stones of pre-historic British sites have often come to be linked with the Arthurian legend. Examples are the megalithic tombs of Arthur's Stone in Herefordshire and

Penllech Coeten Arthur on the Lleyn peninsula, and Cerrig Arthur stone circle near Barmouth, North Wales. The Bronze Age stone circle, the Rollwright Stones, in Oxfordshire has a huge outlying stone called the King Stone. Nearby, the remaining stones of a large megalithic tomb have been dubbed the Whispering Knights in local folklore.

Excalibur

The famous sword of King Arthur is one of the most instantly recognisable elements of the legends and romances. Geoffrey of Monmouth refers to 'his peerless sword, called Caliburn which was forged in the Isle of Avalon'. This then is no ordinary weapon but one created in a magical Otherworld realm where Arthur is taken following his last great battle. In Malory's *Morte d'Arthur* the King commands Sir Bedivere to cast Excalibur into a nearby lake. Bedivere leaves to follow his instructions but finds himself unable to throw the wondrous sword into the waters. He hides it under a tree and returns to Arthur who asks him what he saw when he cast Excalibur away. Bedivere replies that he saw nothing and Arthur commands him to return to the lake and complete the task. For a second time he cannot do as the King commands and repeats that he saw nothing when questioned. Arthur grows angry and insists that Bedivere complete the task which finally and reluctantly he does. On casting the sword into the lake he is amazed to see an arm reach out of the water and catch Excalibur. It brandishes the sword in the air before vanishing beneath the waves. This is generally regarded as an imaginative invention of Malory's but nonetheless it has strong echoes of Celtic water goddess worship and the practice of votive offerings described in Chapter One.

In terms of actual locations in Britain where this is reputed to have taken place, Dozmary Pool on Bodmin Moor, Cornwall, has become associated in legend with these events. As with almost every aspect of the Arthurian stories, however, controversy has raged over exact locations and indeed historical dates.

The poet Alfred, Lord Tennyson, set his *Idylls of the King* in Northern England and associated this story with the Lake District.

Camelot

There has been a variety of claims about the exact location of the legendary court of King Arthur in which the Round Table was said to be housed. Camelot in popular culture is a place of the imagination but, once again, it is likely to have its basis in reality. Many have come to regard South Cadbury Hill Fort in Dorset as a probable setting for Camelot and archaeological excavations by Leslie Alcock between 1966 and 1970 have been interpreted as corroborative evidence for this claim. In 1542 the antiquarian John Leland recorded that South Cadbury was the site of Camelot but needless to say, this has been hotly disputed by historians and archaeologists. Alcock's excavations revealed that this hill fort, which had been in use in one form or another since the Neolithic age, had been re-fortified in the later part of the 5th century AD. This brings the history of the site in line with the likely time period in which Arthur might have lived. He also uncovered the postholes of what seemed to have been a great wooden hall on the crown of the hill. However, it must be added that other hill-forts in Southern England were re-fortified and refurbished during this period.

Camelot is generally described as Arthur's headquarters rather than the capital of Britain. It is tempting to interpret this as suggesting that it was a military base, perhaps one incorporating a town or settlement with which Arthur had strong links. Malory set Camelot in Winchester and similar claims have been made for Caerleon in Monmouthshire, South Wales, Camelford near Tintagel, Cornwall and the ruined Romano-British city of Viriconium or Wroxeter in Shropshire, close to the current Welsh border. Another more northerly location has been suggested at a fort on Hadrian's Wall. If nothing else, these conflicting claims provide further evidence of the widespread nature of Arthur's fame and the repute of his court.

Isle of Avalon

Once again Geoffrey of Monmouth can be considered instrumental in establishing one of the key ingredients in the legends surrounding King Arthur, since it was Geoffrey who first described him being taken to the Isle of Avalon. Malory developed the theme by portraying Arthur, seriously wounded after his battle with his nephew Mordred, being carried away on a barge by the enchantress Morgan le Fay and her female company. In the myths the Isle of Avalon is seen as very much the domain of women. Geoffrey describes it as being ruled over by nine mysterious priestesses and this may echo Celtic accounts of an island off the coast of Brittany that was the sacred enclosure of a company of nine female Druids. The Isle de Seine was a magical place and female Druids were associated with curative and medicinal skills and knowledge.

The concept of Avalon seems to have its basis in the Celtic myths about paradisal Otherworld islands where illness and want are unknown. Avalon is also known as the Island of Apples and the rich orchards surrounding Glastonbury lent further credence to the claims by the monks of the Abbey that the two places were in fact one and the same. In earlier Welsh literature there is reference to an 'Ynis Avallach,' which means Isle of Apples. It is the dwelling place of Avallach, who has been interpreted as either a Celtic deity or a remote ancestral figure. Importantly it is just such a wondrous land as Avalon and is sometimes referred to as the 'Fortunate Isle'. Those who live there are fed by the fruit trees that grow on the island. They are also said to live extremely long lives lasting hundreds of years. This has echoes of the claims that Arthur did not die but his life was magically extended and he is waiting to return either on the Isle of Avalon or in a cave.

Links have been made with the old Welsh term for apple, 'aballon', and Avallach. In the modern Welsh language the word for apple is 'afal'. Whether there has been confusion in the various translations of these myths or there is a genuine linguistic link, apples and Avalon have become inextricably tied together in the popular imagination. In mythology the apple is a fruit that is often connected with the theme of immortality. One of the twelve labours of Hercules was to gather the golden apples of the Hesperides for King Eurystheus. This was as punishment from Apollo for killing his own children when he was driven into madness by the goddess Hera.

The apples were said to be able to give eternal life. They were given as a wedding gift to Zeus and Hera by the Goddess Ge. Hera planted them in the land where the God Atlas stood, holding the world on his shoulders. The tree was guarded by four Nymphs called the Hesperides. They were called Erytheia, Aegle, Arethusa and Hesperia. A terrible dragon watched over the tree. Knowing that the path to the apple tree was beset with great dangers Hercules persuaded Atlas to fetch them whilst he supported the world in his absence. Atlas decided he did not want to carry the world any longer and refused to take it back from Hercules. Hercules agreed to support the world but asked Atlas to take it from him for a while so that he could get a cushion for his neck. Atlas took back the earth but Hercules tricked him and ran away with the apples. Hercules carried them back to King Eurystheus who gave them to the Goddess Athena. Perversely, she chose to hang them back on the tree of the Hesperides. Many elements in this story – the theme of immortality in connection with magical apples, an Otherworld inhabited by a company of mysterious women and the hero's quest connected to a divine authority or deity – reflect aspects of the imagery of Avalon.

Wild Merlin himself is said to have written an old Welsh poem about an apple tree during his period of madness in the forest. In it he says, 'Sweet Apple tree which grows on a river bank / While I was in my right mind I used to have at its foot / A fair wanton maiden, one slender and queenly . . . ' (Merlin and Wales, quoted in Michael Dames, *A Magician's Landscape*, p123.) The poem equates the apple tree with a beautiful woman and the subject of love. The apple is often seen as symbolic of sexual love. Most famously, of course, it is the fruit with which

Eve tempts Adam in the Garden of Eden. This suggests an already established link between apples and sex in Pre-Christian cultures. Outside of a Christian context it is more usually linked to fertility and fecundity. In Norse mythology for example the apples of perpetual youth are said to grow in Asgard.

5

GRAIL MYSTERIES

The Templars

The Templars have proven to be as fertile a subject matter for the imagination as the Grail itself. Authors and historians often seem to fall into two distinct camps when relating their story. Some view them simply as a military order of warrior monks formed in the political and religious context of the crusades of the Middle Ages, whilst others view them as having been an altogether more mysterious and secretive organisation. Perhaps most dramatically some have claimed that they were the guardians of the Holy Grail, although, in recent years, there has been intense speculation about what the Grail was actually intended to represent.

In order to explore these intriguing claims it is necessary to give a short account of the orthodox history of the order. According to the medieval chronicler William of Tyre, the Templars were formed in 1119. A group of nine knights led by Hugh of Payns had approached the King of Jerusalem, Baldwin II, to seek his permission to found a military group who would follow the rule of a religious order but who would undertake the responsibility of protecting pilgrims arriving in and travelling through the Holy Land. Their request was granted and they were given quarters in the al-Aqsa mosque that stood on the southern edge of the Temple Mount in Jerusalem. This building was reputed to be built on the site of the Temple of Solomon. Originally they were known as the 'Poor Fellow-Soldiers of Jesus Christ'. From their living quarters they became known as 'The Knights of the Temple of Solomon', and from this derives the better-known name of the Templars. The idea of their poverty is reflected in their official seal, which often depicted two knights having to ride one horse. However, the Templars became an extremely wealthy and powerful organisation and were given many generous donations by important patrons and granted special rights by the Pope himself. This was to prove especially significant in that they were answerable only to the Pope and were effectively beyond the control of any secular ruler.

In the nearly two hundred years of the existence of their order they gained lands throughout Europe and became important mediators and influential advisors to the powerful figures of their age. They also developed the first banking system in Christian culture that enabled pilgrims to make deposits at the start of their journey and withdraw money at its end. Their role as international bankers and the great wealth they enjoyed as a result of donations and special privileges meant they became the object of envy and resentment from many quarters. King Philip IV of France, known as Philip the Fair, envied both their wealth and power and, faced by money problems of his own, he declared them heretics, largely in order to be able to seize their assets, and forced the reluctant Pope Clement V to support his action against them in 1307. Terrible charges were made against the Templars that included heresy, denying the cross, worshipping obscene idols and homosexuality. They were alleged by the Inquisition to have given particular importance to an idol in the form of a severed head that was referred to as 'Baphomet'. In 1312 the order was suppressed by Pope Clement V and the Grand Master, Jacques de Molay, together with the Preceptor of

Normandy, Geoffrey of Charney, were burnt to death as heretics in 1314.

The accusations brought against them by the Inquisition may be one of the sources of the recurrent myths connecting the Templars with the Grail. The reliability of such claims is of course open to question given the nature of the Inquisition and its terrifying modes of questioning. However, some of the charges made against the Templars are intriguing within the context of the story of the Grail.

'Item, that in each province they had idols, namely heads, of which some had three faces, and some one, and others had a human skull.

> Item, that they adored these idols, or that idol, and especially in their great chapters and assemblies . . .
> Item, that they said that the heads could save them.
> Item, that (it could) make riches . . .
> Item, that it made the trees flower.
> Item, that (it made) the land germinate.'
>> (Quoted in Keith Laidler, *The Head of God*, p222.)

Keith Laidler has pointed out the similarities between the heads that the Templars are said to have adored and the Holy Grail which is described in the Grail romances as having the power to heal the land and make the trees flower. He develops an unorthodox hypothesis that the head of Baphomet is in fact the embalmed head of Jesus found beneath the Temple of Solomon by the Templars during secret excavations there and that the head and the Grail are one and the same.

Another contributing cause for the identification of the Templars with the Grail is Wolfram von Eschenbach's *Parzival*. In the romance of the German writer the Grail is kept in a temple and its Guardians are known as 'templeise'. Many people have interpreted this term as referring to the Templars and have argued that the order of the Grail knights that he depicts is a thinly veiled representation of them. However, the

Templars were not a particularly well-known or established order in Germany at the time that Wolfram was writing. Because of this and the lack of any other evidence in the text that he is clearly referring to the Templars, orthodox historians have largely dismissed this claim.

The Cathars

The Cathars were another heretical sect of the Middle Ages who were to become associated with the Grail and about whom there is a good deal of speculative thought. Catharism was a divergent form of Christianity that gained a great deal of popular support from the nobility of the South of France and the general population, particularly in the Languedoc-Roussillon region, between 1142 and around 1250.

They named themselves 'Cathari', meaning 'pure', and strove to achieve lives of spiritual perfection. Many within the Cathar movement felt that the Roman Catholic Church was corrupt and influenced by material greed, which may help to explain the appeal of Catharism amongst the ordinary people of Southern France. They were also known as the Albigensians after the town of Albi which was particularly sympathetic to their cause. One of the ways in which they diverged from orthodox Catholicism was in their rejection of institutional religious hierarchy and the idea that God could only be approached through the clergy. Cathars strove instead for a direct, individual, mystical awareness of God. However, they did have religious leaders known as *perfecti* or 'perfect ones', who acted as spiritual advisors, but, compared to the Roman Catholic Church, they conducted little in the way of religious ceremonies. They also eschewed church buildings for their services and meetings and instead would conduct them in the open air, or 'everyday' settings such as people's houses or barns. It is thought that Catharism was descended from Gnostic traditions that argued that it was possible to achieve an ultimate spiritual union with God. Gnosis is the Greek word for an inner 'knowing'. This early Christian tradition put the emphasis on the responsibility of the individual to achieve spiritual growth and awareness, undermining and contradicting Roman Catholic dogma and power. The Cathars had a dualistic worldview in which a 'good' God and his evil son were in a constant state of conflict. The first men were said to be angels who had been trapped by the evil God in the material world. These men, although made of corrupt and evil matter, were essentially good. In order to become re-united with the good God and the world of light from which they had come, they undertook a rigorous path to spiritual enlightenment that involved fasting and the attempt to live lives of purity.

The Cathars, like the Gnostics, also believed in a feminine aspect of God or the Godhead and Cathar *perfecti* were often female. Once again this was in direct conflict with the patriarchal structure of the Catholic Church. This feminine influence can be found in the Gnostic Gospels, a collection of early Christian texts in which the Holy Spirit found in the Trinity appears to be female.

The Cathars' attitude towards Jesus Christ has led many historians to argue that they are an unlikely religious group to link with the Grail. Although they recognised and worshipped him as a sacred figure they did not believe that humanity had been redeemed by his death on the cross. His importance lay in his message of love and his physical death reflected the real nature of the world. Although they believed he was a messenger from the good God they did not believe in the virgin birth and argued that resurrection of the soul must happen in life and not after death. However, as a messenger of love, Christ was a sacred figure to the Cathars and items connected with his life, like the Grail, would have been of sacred value. In many ways the beliefs of the Cathars can be seen to reflect the values of the Grail knights. By living pure and spiritual lives and undertaking individual journeys to reach an ultimate goal which involved a mystical communion with God they appear to share many of the same values. It has been argued that the concept of courtly love and the Grail quest were in fact veiled reflections of the Cathar faith. As we saw in Chapter Two, Chrétien de Troyes was attached to the court of Eleanor of Aquitaine and Marie de Champagne who were powerful and influential figures from the nobility of the South of France. It is argued by some scholars that their influence and ideals were reflected in the work that Chrétien wrote for them.

There have been similar claims about the work of the troubadours who expounded the subject of courtly love. The theme of the love triangle is interpreted as having an underlying symbolism. The jealous husband represented the clergy and the object of their devotion was their 'lady church' and the worship of the female aspect of divinity.

In responding to the widespread and heretical beliefs of the Cathars, Pope Innocent III was responsible for launching the first crusade with Christians as its target. The Albigensian Crusade, as it came to be known, followed failed attempts by Innocent to pressure the nobility of the South of France into dealing with the Cathar movement. He offered all who would participate in this crusade forgiveness of all sins committed and the far more appealing promise that the lands taken during this action would be given to the victors. Given such generous terms the northern nobility of France, who had long been jealous of their richer and more cultured counterparts in the south, rapidly assembled in pursuit of lands and booty. In 1209 an army of Northern crusaders formed at Lyons and marched on the Languedoc region. The crusade was to be astonishing in its cruelty and barbarity. In the city of Béziers up to 15,000 people, including women and children, were murdered. Many more cities were attacked and fell to the crusaders but the Cathars fought back and resistance to the servants of the Catholic Church was fierce.

The struggle was to continue for decades and, in 1243, the final stronghold of the Cathars, a mountain fortress called Montségur, was besieged by an army from the nearby city of Carcassonne fighting on behalf of King Louis of France and the Pope. Montségur translates as 'Mount Safe' and was a formidable fortress placed high on a tall peak amongst the Pyrenean foothills. Its reputation as a military base, whose geographical features made it extremely difficult to attack, was matched by the tales of Cathar treasure that was said to be held there. Such rumours no doubt helped persuade many to participate in the action against it. One of the items said to be part of the Cathar treasure was a 'rich cup' which was used in one of their ceremonies, the *manisola*. This ceremony involved a religious feast in which such a cup was said to be passed around the assembled company drawing parallels with the Grail knights and the Fisher King who is fed by the Grail. The nature of the Cathar treasure, which was never recovered, has been the subject of much speculation. When Montségur finally fell in 1244 the material and religious treasures of the Cathars had vanished. If, indeed, they had ever existed.

Rosslyn Chapel
Although the Knights Templar had been brutally suppressed in France there is some evidence to suggest that the higher echelons of the order had some advance warning of the imminent danger that they were in. During questioning by the Inquisition Jean de Chalons, the Preceptor of France, stated that a group of Templars had fled Paris with the treasure of the order and had travelled to the harbour of La Rochelle. The order had a fleet of eighteen galleys onto which the treasure was loaded. The escaping group of Templars then set out to sea. It is certainly true that the forces of the French king never captured the records and alleged religious treasures of the order.

The fleet is said to have split in two and one group headed south to Portugal where they found sanctuary. The king of Portugal did not persecute them and the order evolved and underwent a change of name as a means of escaping the wrath of the Pope. The second part of the fleet is said to have sailed to Scotland and landed near Edinburgh. As an order the Templars had been established in Scotland from its earliest days and had land and holdings there. They also had very strong links with the Saint-Claire family. One of the key founders of the order, Hugh de Payns, had married into the family and built a Templar preceptory on lands owned by them. At the time of their arrival in 1307, Robert the Bruce had been excommunicated by the Pope and Keith Laidler has argued that this made Scotland an ideal choice for the order at this time and that they pledged allegiance to his cause.

The strong links between the Templars and Saint-Claire or later Sinclair family has focused attention on an unusual chapel that was built at Rosslyn in 1446. Built on the instructions of Sir William Sinclair, the third Earl of Orkney, it has been regarded as exceptional and eccentric by some and un-Christian and idolatrous by others. The chapel is remarkable not for its size or scale but for the imagery and iconography that it contains. It combines stone carvings drawn from pagan, Celtic and Judaic sources with biblical images that have been the source of much speculation. Amongst the multitude of Green men carvings, representing a Pagan fertility deity, the image of the Grail as a chalice cup appears many times on the ceiling and walls of the chapel. The depiction of the Grail in this context has become the source of considerable conjecture. Rosslyn Chapel itself has at times in its history been the subject of religious controversy. Indeed in 1592 the Chapel was de-consecrated as a place of Christian worship on the basis of the imagery contained within it. The Chapel was not re-consecrated until 1862. It is claimed that many Templar symbols are contained within the Chapel and that it was built to house the treasure of the order carried to Scotland from France. Baigent, Leigh and Lincoln argued in their book *The Holy Blood and the Holy Grail* that the Templars were sympathetic to the Cathars as they both apparently shared Gnostic beliefs and it has been suggested that they may have become guardians of their knowledge or treasure following the fall of Montségur.

Whatever form the Grail is alleged to have taken, the traditional chalice or a preserved head as Keith Laidler has suggested, Rosslyn Chapel has been claimed by many to be its final resting place. Within the Chapel itself one feature, called the Apprentice pillar, has particularly drawn the attention of researchers on the subject of the Grail. The pillar has an unusual combination of religious imagery. The main body of the stone pillar is covered in a spiral pattern of leaves that is said by official chroniclers of the Chapel to represent the Tree of Life, a well-known allusion to Jesus. At its base are coiled eight serpents. At the top of the column is a scene said to show the biblical story of Abraham who nearly sacrifices his son Isaac before God intervenes and a ram is sacrificed in his place. Local legend states that the Grail is hidden within the pillar. Some have interpreted the pillar as representing Yggdrasil the Nordic World Tree with the Niddhagg serpent at its base. Although the pillar has been scanned by radar no hollow features were revealed. However conjecture has pointed to the sealed vaults of the Chapel and the floor directly beneath the Apprentice pillar. In 2001 excavations took place within the Chapel vaults revealing several burials but nothing more.

Rennes-le-Chateau

One of the most popular and unorthodox theories relating to the Grail to emerge in the last few decades has focused on the small French village of Rennes-Le-Chateau. Located in the South of France near the Pyrenees and close to the ancient Cathar stronghold of Montségur, it is a seemingly remote and rural backwater. The village achieved an international notoriety following the publication in 1982 of *The Holy Blood and the Holy Grail* by Michael Baigent, Richard Leigh & Henry Lincoln. They had investigated a series of mysterious events that had taken place at Rennes-Le-Chateau. Their research resulted in a controversial theory that many were to find both shocking and disturbing.

Their investigation concerned a parish priest of the village called Bérenger Saunière who had taken up his post in 1885. Between 1885 and 1891 he appears to have been a conventional local priest who survived on a modest income and had a keen interest in the history of the local area. However, in 1891, whilst carrying out restoration to restore the village church, he is said to have discovered a number of parchments concealed in a hollow pillar. These are claimed to have comprised a series of genealogies and a cryptic cipher. Following this discovery the priest experienced a mysterious increase in wealth that he appears to have spent carrying out lavish and bizarre building work including an eccentric Tower of the Magdalene, and on refurbishment of the church. The priest is said to have only shared the secret of his wealth with his housekeeper and companion, Marie Dernaud and this led to considerable speculation about its source. To add to the bizarre nature of the tale, Saunière was denied the last rites and absolution following his final confession on his deathbed by the attending priest. This led to the belief that he might have been privy to some shocking information that threatened the church and that his money had come through blackmail. Dernaud died in 1953 without revealing the secret of Saunière's wealth. Rumours grew that he may have found the mythical lost Cathar treasure, which could have included the Holy Grail, or gold buried by the Visigoths who had once dominated the region.

Baigent, Leigh and Lincoln, in the course of their researches, conceived the hypothesis that the genealogies found by Saunière demonstrated that Jesus and Mary Magdalene had in fact married and had children. Those descendants married into Visigoth society and created a royal line of kings known as the Merovingians.

According to Baigent, Leigh and Lincoln, the Holy Grail was essentially a coded reference to a royal bloodline. In one 15th century romance by John Hardyng the Holy Grail is described as the 'san greal', which, in the slightly modified version of 'sang real', translates as 'royal blood'. Critics have argued that this is most likely to be the result of an error of translation or transcription rather than a reference to the passing on of a secret history. However, their investigations led them to conclude that a secret society connected to the Templars called the Prieuré de Sion had been privy to this knowledge for centuries. The evidence put forward by them, and many subsequent writers, involves a vast, concealed conspiracy theory that is connected to an astonishing range of historical figures and events. A whole plethora of books have resulted from this hypothesis and it has recently formed the basis for the bestselling novel, *The Da Vinci Code* by Dan Brown.

The Turin Shroud

The Turin Shroud is reputed to be the burial shroud that Jesus was wrapped in following the crucifixion. It is a 14-foot piece of linen which appears to show the ghostly impression of a long haired, bearded man who has injuries consistent with his having been crucified. Opinion has veered wildly as to its authenticity and speculation continues to the present day.

The shroud was first documented in a written source in 1357. It was put on display as the actual burial shroud of Christ in a church in the French town of Lirey. It has been conjectured by writers and historians such as Ian Wilson that it was the same piece of cloth known in the 4th century as the Edessa burial sheet. (Edessa is known today as Urfa in Turkey.) This shroud was believed to be the cloth that Joseph of Arimathea had bought for the burial of Jesus.

The Edessa cloth was said to have an imprint of the body of Christ. Documents from this time describe it as an item of great veneration that was shown rarely and only on important occasions. The shroud was said to have been taken to Constantinople in 944. Shroud researcher Daniel C Scavone has argued that the earliest documents regarding the Edessa burial sheet indicate that it was stored in a rectangular box and was a 'tetradiplon', meaning it was folded in eight layers. He suggests that the cloth was kept folded so that only the head of Jesus was visible through a glass panel and that this was painted by Byzantine religious artists. Until 1204 the shroud was rarely exhibited and Scavone argues that at this time, when the Fourth Crusade was underway, rumours of this sacred icon, associated with the death and blood of Christ and linked to Joseph of Arimathea, began to spread back to Western Europe. He speculates that this may have in some way found echoes in the Celtic tale of the head of Bran the Blessed carried on a dish swimming with blood and said to have supernatural powers.

Scavone argues that it is the shroud, linked both to Joseph of Arimathea and to the crucifixion, that was the source and inspiration for the romances of the Holy Grail. He also argues that the word 'Grail' derives from the Latin 'gradalis' meaning 'by degrees'. The shroud was referred to in this way because it may have been displayed in stages, pulled upwards out of the case and unfolded during religious ceremonies.

The shroud that was displayed in Lirey was recorded as belonging to a man named Geoffrey de Charnay. In his book *The Turin Shroud* (1978), Ian Wilson conjectured that he may have been a descendant of a Templar knight of the same name who acquired the shroud during the crusades. He drew parallels with the alleged Templar ceremonies featuring a sacred head and the appearance of the shroud in its case. If there was a family link between the Geoffrey de Charney who owned the shroud and the order it would help to explain the stories and legends that describe the Templars as being guardians of the Grail. The shroud was first taken to Turin cathedral in 1578 and from there it gained its current name.

When an attempt was made in 1988 to establish the age of the shroud through carbon dating it appeared to show that it could not date from the time of Christ. It dated the fabric of the shroud to between 1260 and 1390. However, critics including Ian Wilson have argued that the sample taken from the shroud for testing may not have been part of the main body of the original cloth and was therefore contaminated.

The shroud has caused controversy from its earliest recorded display and it has been banned by the Catholic Church at various points and been declared a hoax by many. It has been said to be a photographic image created by Leonardo Da Vinci (the theory that Da Vinci created the image using a photographic technique was put forward by Lynn Picknett and Clive Prince in their book *The Turin Shroud: In Whose Image?*) and claimed to have healing, curative properties. It continues to polarise debate and drew an audience of more than three million people when it was displayed in 2000. It will next be shown to the public in 2025.

> 'The shroud is an image of God's love as well as of human sin. The imprint left by the tortured body of the Crucified One, which attests to the tremendous human capacity for causing pain and death to one's fellow man, stands as an icon of the suffering of the innocent in every age.'

In 2000 Pope John Paul II decided that the Turin Shroud's next exhibition would be in Turin in 2025, to coincide with the next Holy Year of the Roman Catholic Church. Pope Benedict XVI then announced on 2nd June 2008, that the Archbishop of Turin had requested that the date for its next scheduled display be moved forward. Pope Benedict agreed to this, and a press release was issued the next day from the keepers of the Shroud in Turin. The press release revealed that the purpose of the exhibition was to focus on pastoral issues, and to allow pilgrims to see it for the first time since having undergone restoration in 2002. Restoration had caused dismay amongst many, who alleged that the appearance of the cloth had been altered in the process. The press release also announced that no further testing of the Shroud would be allowed during the 2010 exhibition. On Saturday 10th April 2010, the Turin Shroud went on display to the public in the Cathedral of St John the Baptist in Turin, Italy. This is the eighteenth time in its recorded history that the shroud has been exhibited to the general public.

Researcher Dr Barbara Frale, who works for the Vatican and therefore has access to the Vatican Secret Archives, has made a number of interesting statements regarding the Shroud in recent times. With Vatican support and access to contemporary documents, Frale carried out a study of the trial of the Knights Templar. A document known as the Chinon Parchment led Frale's study to dramatic conclusions. Most notable among these is that a Vatican trial conducted at the time of the Templars' arrest in France actually found them to be innocent, and that the King of France had demanded that the verdict be suppressed – forcing Pope Clement V to follow his wishes.

Frale discovered the record of the trial of the Templars in 2003 after realising that it had been wrongly catalogued within the Vatican archives. Although Pope Clement V had found them guilty of a number of grave sins, including sexual immorality and corruption, they were ultimately declared innocent of the more serious charge of heresy. Interestingly, it emerges that one aspect of their initiation ceremony involved being told to spit on the cross. This act was not designed to be heretical, but to prepare initiates for what they might be forced to do if captured by Muslim forces. This act may also have been designed to test discipline. Dr Barbara Frale published a book on her findings, *The Templars: The Secret History Revealed*, in 2009.

An article printed in *The Times* newspaper on the 6th April 2009 reported that Frale had also unearthed new evidence that the Turin Shroud had been in the possession of the Knights Templar. According to the Vatican researcher, the Knights Templar had retained the Shroud following the sack of Constantinople in 1204, venerating it and using it in initiation rituals. In studying the trial of the Templars, Frale discovered a document that contained the testimony of a French knight called Arnaut Sabbatier. Sabbatier joined the order in 1287 and described how, during his initiation ceremony, he was taken to 'a secret place to which only the brothers of the Temple had access'. He then recounted that he was shown 'a long linen cloth on which was impressed the figure of a man' and told to venerate the image and kiss the feet of the figure three times. In light of this testimony, Frale draws attention to the trial of the Templars on charges of heresy, and in particular the accusation that they had worshipped a bearded figure. She argued that this was in fact a misrepresented reference to their worship of the Turin Shroud.

An article published in *The Times* newspaper on the 21st November 2009 reported Dr Frale's claim to have deciphered the 'burial certificate of Jesus the Nazarene, or Jesus of Nazareth' imprinted on the Turin Shroud. Frale allegedly reconstructed the death certificate from fragments of Greek, Hebrew and Latin writing found on the cloth. The writing is apparently not obvious to the human eye. As with the image of the man on the Shroud, the writing appears in reverse, and can therefore be most clearly deciphered in a negative photograph. Other scholars have argued that the writing comes from a reliquary that was attached to the cloth during the medieval period. In response, Frale argued that a medieval Christian would not have used the term 'the Nazarene' because it would have been deemed heretical to refer to Jesus as a man as opposed to the Son of God. Speaking to *La Repubblicca*, Frale said that at the time of Christ, Jewish custom dictated that in a Roman colony such as Palestine, a body that had been buried after a death sentence had to spend one year in a communal grave before being returned to their family. In order to identify the body, a death certificate was glued to the burial shroud. The certificate was usually attached to the head or face of the shroud covering the body. This account differs from the Biblical account of the burial of Christ, which stipulates that Christ was buried in the tomb provided by Joseph of Arimathea.

Frale's reconstruction of the death certificate reads as follows:

In the year 16 of the reign of the Emperor Tiberius Jesus the Nazarene, taken down in the early evening after having been condemned to death by a Roman judge because he was found guilty by a Hebrew authority, is hereby sent for burial with the obligation of being consigned to his family only after one full year.

According to Frale, the use of three different languages was a result of the multi-lingual society created by Greek-speaking Jews living in a Roman colony.

With specific reference to the Turin Shroud, Frale argues that legends that claim the Templars as the guardians of the Holy Grail might have some basis in historical truth. She also supports the idea (disputed by authors such as Richard Barber) that the German poet Wolfram von Eschenbach represents the Templars as the keepers of the Grail in his version of the 13th century epic poem *Parzifal*.

In her book *The Templars: The Secret History Revealed* (p201) Frale puts forth other ideas in relation to the Templars. These include that the Templars participated in a special rite of the Passion of Christ that was celebrated on the evening of Holy Thursday. This rite was celebrated in commemoration of the Last Supper. Notably, she argues that the Templars probably only received communion in the form of wine (representing the blood of Christ). According to Frale, this practice was unknown in the Roman Catholic Church and is currently being researched by a number of Byzantine scholars at the Pontifical Oriental Institute in Rome. It is speculated that this practice was used only by the Templars, and that it drew on ancient traditions based in Jerusalem with roots in the early Christian church. Frale then hypothesizes that this might have influenced ideas concerning the Grail, including stories such as those of Robert de Boron.

De Boron endorses the idea, for example, that the Holy Grail is said to be the cup that Jesus used at the Last Supper, thereby beginning the celebration of the Eucharist, as well as being the same cup in which Joseph of Arimathea caught the blood of Christ. Frale concludes that such ideas are 'certainly legitimate speculation, but in the absence of reliable proof a historian must go no further than the simple presentation of the facts.' (Barbara Frale, *The Templars: The Secret History Revealed*, p202)

The Sudarium of Oviedo

The argument that the Turin Shroud is older than scientific tests suggest is supported by its alleged relationship to another famous Christian relic, the Sudarium of Oviedo (or the Shroud of Oviedo). This small piece of linen stained with blood is believed by some to be one of the burial cloths used to cover the body of Jesus. The burial cloths are described in the New Testament in the Gospel of John as follows:

'Then Simon Peter came, following him, and went into the tomb. He saw the linen wrappings lying there, and the cloth that had been on Jesus' head, not lying with the linen wrappings but rolled up in a place by itself.' (John 20:6–7)

Measuring 84 x 53 centimetres, and known by its Latin name, *Sudarium* ('sweat cloth'), the sacred piece of cloth is held in a small chapel called the Camara Santa of the Cathedral of San Salvador in the city of Oviedo in northern Spain. It is believed by many that the cloth was placed over the face of Jesus after his death on the cross.

The small chapel that contains the sacred cloth was said to have been built purposefully to house it in AD 840 by King Alonso II of Asturias. The chapel is, for example, referred to by Antoninus of Piacenza, a 6th century pilgrim to the Holy Land who described places and relics of religious importance.

While Antoninus Piacenza's reliability has in the past been disputed, his accounts are viewed as significant because he was amongst the last to travel in Palestine while it was still under the control of the Christian Byzantine Empire. In AD 570, Antoninus recorded that the Sudarium was held near Jerusalem in a cave close to the Monastery of Saint Mark. However, following the invasion of the region and subsequent capture of Jerusalem by the Sassanid King of Persia, Chosroes II, the Sudarium was removed in AD 614 in order to protect it.

It is thought that the Sudarium was carried, away from the threat of invading Persian forces, through North Africa, perhaps via Alexandria. Its estimated date of arrival in Spain is around AD 616. It appeared for a time in Seville and Toledo until being carried further north to the city of Oviedo, away from expanding Muslim power, in AD 718. Scientists who carried out tests on the Sudarium have observed that the Sudarium and Turin Shroud share many common features.

Mark Guscin's 1999 report describes the results of these scientific tests. Amongst the similarities noted between the Sudarium and the Shroud, Guscin points out that tests on the two cloths show that the bloodstains belonged to the same blood group, AB. The Shroud and the Sudarium also contain Pollen grains from a plant that grows in an area between Lebanon and Jerusalem. Both cloths appear also to have at some point covered a victim who had been tortured and died in a manner consistent with crucifixion. Perhaps most importantly though, the blood stains on the Sudarium match those on the Shroud. Further investigation revealed that the Sudarium had covered the head of a man in a vertical position, which was then removed before the burial shroud was laid over his face.

In conclusion, Guscin argues that if (as the research appeared to show) both cloths had covered the corpse of the same man at about the same time, then this would imply that scientists and historians who date the Turin Shroud to the 14th century are inaccurate, and that the Turin Shroud must be at least as old as the known history of the Sudarium of Oviedo. The combination of scientific findings and available historical documents therefore suggest the possibility that the Shroud and the Sudarium both originated in Jerusalem in the 1st century AD. However, this report is of course not without its critics, and sceptics have argued that some of the scientific methodology used to conduct testing on the cloths is flawed.

The Virgin and the Grail

Joseph Goering has arguably produced one of the most sober and plausible theories concerning the origins of the Grail romances in recent years. Goering, a professor at the University of Toronto in Canada, produced a cautious and scholarly work called *The Virgin and the Grail* that was published by Yale University Press in 2005. In it he argues that the inspiration for the very first known Grail romance by 12th century French poet Chrétien de Troyes, came from a painting.

Goering draws parallels between Chrétien's depiction of the Grail as a shallow serving dish, or plate, that shines brightly while being carried in a mysterious procession through the court of the Fisher King, and religious wall paintings from a remote region of the eastern Pyrenees. These wall paintings, created in churches during the first half of the 12th century and thus pre-dating Chrétien's story, depict the Virgin Mary holding a mysterious vessel whose form varies from painting to painting in her covered hand. Georing's work identifies a specific image from this sequence of Romanesque artworks in which Mary is holding a shallow dish that appears to be emitting mysterious, fiery rays.

The specific image is located in the Church of St Clement, in Tahull, the Diocese of Roda. The Church of St Clement was consecrated by Bishop Raymund of Roda in December 1123. The event was recorded for posterity on a column within the church and also in the *Book of St Raymund*, a parchment volume consisting of 225 folios (550 pages). The church's paintings would have been executed in preparation for its consecration by the Bishop. Although unknown artists produced the paintings, the painter responsible for the unusual image of the Virgin Mary is generally referred to as the Master of St Clement.

The paintings were removed from the church during the early 20th century and are now preserved at the National Museum of the Art of Catalonia in Barcelona. Goering argues that the context of the image is very important because the

Virgin Mary is portrayed as the head of the Apostolic College. The apostles are depicted beneath the dominant image of Christ in Majesty, who is encircled by the four evangelists: Matthew, Mark, Luke and John. Below the evangelists are St Mary and St John. Mary is flanked by St Bartholomew and St Thomas, while St John is flanked by St James. Unfortunately, for various reasons, the original paintings of other apostles have been covered or lost.

The figure of the Virgin Mary is dressed in a white wimple (a style of headdress) and is wearing a white and red cloth around her shoulders. Her right hand is extended palm upwards to the viewer. It is significant that she is holding the aforementioned shallow dish with her left hand enfolded in her cloak. This is significant because it resonates with a traditional artistic tradition of Christian images that signify that the object is considered to be sacred or holy. The shallow dish is giving off mysterious rays of light or fire.

Goering argues that the fresco evokes the Biblical events of the Feast of Pentecost. The Feast of Pentecost takes place fifty days after Easter Sunday, when Christ was resurrected after the crucifixion and ten days after the Ascension. On that day the Apostles and Mary met together in an upper room in a house in Jerusalem:

> 'And suddenly a sound came from heaven like the rush of a mighty wind, and it filled all the house where they were sitting. And there appeared to them tongues as of fire, distributed and resting on each one of them. And they were filled with the Holy Spirit and began to speak in other tongues, as the Spirit gave them utterance.' (Acts 2:1-4)

According to the Bible, it is following the events of Pentecost that the apostles set off to spread Christ's teachings into the wider world. Goering speculates that the Master of St Clement may have invented the image of the radiant dish to illustrate the idea 'the tongues of fire' and the pouring out of the Holy Spirit at Pentecost. The Apostles who flank the Virgin Mary are depicted holding books. Goering suggests this is likely to symbolise that they are intending to go out and preach as a result of the events of Pentecost. According to Goering, iconography depicting the Virgin holding a variety of different forms of vessels is unique to this region and period, and appears to have not developed further beyond this time and place.

Whilst Goering's study offers an analysis of the early development of the Grail romances and its most important innovators, including Robert de Boron and Wolfram von Eschenbach, he focuses in particular on the first known Grail story, that written by Chrétien de Troyes. In comparing the paintings with Chrétien's story, Goering identifies specific Christian religious practices that may have had an influence on the portrayal de Troyes created of the Grail.

One of the scenes that is depicted in the poem *Perceval, The Story of the Grail*, is of an enigmatic and bizarre procession led by a squire holding a lance. A drop of blood flows from the tip of the lance, and the squire's focus is a wondrous vessel carried in front of the inexperienced young knight, Perceval:

'Then two other squires entered holding in their hands candelabra of pure gold, crafted with enamel inlays. The young men carrying the candelabra were extremely handsome. In each of the candelabra there were at least ten candles burning

A maiden accompanying the two young men was carrying a grail with her two hands; she was beautiful, noble and richly attired. After she had entered the hall carrying the grail the room was so brightly illuminated that the candles lost their brilliance like stars and the moon when the sun rises. After her came another maiden, carrying a silver carving platter. The grail, which was introduced first, was of fine pure gold. Set in the grail were precious stones of many kinds, the best and costliest to be found in earth or sea: the grail's stones were finer than any others in the world, without any doubt.

The grail passed by like the lance; they passed in front of the bed and into another chamber. The young knight watched them pass by but did not dare ask who was served from the grail, for in his heart he always held the wise gentleman's advice.' (*Arthurian Romances*, Chrétien de Troyes, p420–421).

Whilst many have argued that the term 'grail' is derived from the Latin term *gradalis*, meaning 'by degrees', Goering instead suggests that it has its roots in the language of northern Spain (Catalonia) and southern France (Occitania). According to Goering, the earliest record of a similar term is found in a will of 1010, in which Count Ermengol I of Urgell left two silver grails, or *gradales*. In the Catalonian region a serving dish was a piece of tableware referred to as a *gradal*. In Old Occitan, the term *grazala* is used. This translates into Old French as *graal*, which also corresponds to *greal* in Old Castilian. Goering argues that the ultimate root of the word 'grail' resides in the Catalan word *gresa*, meaning potter's clay. Although the term was not well-known in Europe, it does appear in a small number of poems pre-dating Chrétien de Troyes' romance to signify a piece of tableware.

The young knight Perceval learns later in the *Story of the Grail* that his failure to ask who was served from the Grail was a sin, and that his silence has important consequences. A holy hermit whom he encounters in the forest explains to him that,

'The man served from it is my brother. Your mother was his sister and mine; and the rich Fisher King, I believe, is the son of the king who is served from the grail.

And do not imagine he is served pike or lamprey or salmon. A single host that is brought to him in that grail sustains and brings comfort to that holy man-such is the holiness of the grail!' (*Arthurian Romances*, Chrétien de Troyes, p460)

Perceval had previously been warned against talking too much and so remains silent. A hideous damsel warns him that asking the question regarding the Grail would result in healing the wounded king. Chrétien's story suggests that a king who is unable to rule effectively or lead his men into battle endangers the land of being laid waste by the ravages of war. In this sense Chrétien envisages a practical difficulty arising from the condition of the wounded king who is also the father of the Fisher King. Later writers and film-makers such as T. S. Eliot and John Boorman arguably view the concept of the 'wasteland' as a mystical and spiritual doom arising from some form of symbiotic relationship between a medieval king and a landscape.

The story clearly depicts a sense of great mystery surrounding the Grail. However it is also possible that Chrétien intended the real source of awe to be the mystical power of the communion wafer. Perceval also learns, for example, that the crippled father of the Fisher King has been kept alive by the Eucharistic wafer, or host, for twelve years and has not left his chamber in all that time.

Joseph Goering suggests that the mythical figure of Perceval may in fact be based on a real person whose exploits inspired the songs and tales of a jongleur. Although opinion is divided amongst historians and writers, it is possible that a story that featured a hero called Perceval and a Grail was familiar in the south of France before Chrétien de Troyes wrote his tale. At the beginning of *Perceval*, Chrétien writes that his patron Count Philip of Flanders had given him a book that contained the story he was putting into rhyme. This might suggest that de Troyes was in fact working from an extant source.

A poem written by the Occitanian poet Rigaut de Barbezieux contains the following reference:

'Just as Perceval, when he was alive, was lost in wonderment at the sight, so that he could never ask what purpose the lance and the Grail served, so I likewise, Best of Ladies, for I forget all when I gaze on you.' (*The Virgin and the Grail*, p145).

Goering argues that this poem, from *The Virgin and the Grail*, is in fact older than Chrétien de Troyes's *Perceval*. This leads him to endorse the suggestion of a Swiss scholar called Andre de Mandach that the figure of Perceval is based on Count Rotrou II of the Perche region of France.

Rotrou II reigned from 1099–1144. Mandach argues that Perceval was the nickname by which he was known. Located in northern France, 150 kilometres southwest of Paris, the Perche region is famous for producing strong Percheron horses. Goering argues that Rotrou II provides a plausible link between the remote areas of the Pyrenees and the north of France, where Chrétien de Troyes first wrote his Grail story.

Rotrou II himself gained fame and acclaim during his lifetime as a participant on the First Crusade. He set out in September 1096 and was involved in the siege of Nicaea and the siege of Antioch. Chronicles of this time record his bravery at the siege of Antioch of 1098 and link him with the discovery of the Holy Lance.

After capturing Antioch, the Crusaders themselves became besieged and suffered terrible privations of food and sickness. A peasant from Provencal called Peter Bartholomew had a vision in which Christ and St Andrew told him that the Holy Lance that had pierced the side of Christ was buried beneath the altar of St Peter's in Antioch. Miraculously, the Holy Lance was discovered by the Crusaders on the evening of the 14th June. Whether or not this was a real miracle or a carefully stage-managed event, the discovery of the Holy Lance proved to be a great morale boost for the struggling Crusaders. On the 28th June, the Lance was carried into battle and the crusader army drove off the besieging forces, allegedly aided by warrior saints such as St George. Rotrou was a commander during this battle and later poems record the event.

After returning home to Europe, Rotrou enjoyed success as the Count of the Perche. In recognition of his achievements on Crusade, he was offered the hand in marriage of Matilda, the daughter of Henry I of England. Rotrou was also the cousin of Alfonso I, King of Aragon. From about 1108, he helped his cousin fight against Muslim armies in Spain. Goering argues that his links with Alfonso would have meant that Rotrou would have been familiar with the region from where the Grail paintings of the Pyrenees originate. Moreover, it transpires that he also knew Bishop Raymund of Roda, who consecrated the Church of St Clement at Tahull. In Catalan, Rotrou was known as 'Conde de Alperche', and Goering suggests that in Occitania he might have been known as 'Valperche' or 'perche-Val'.

Given that the count therefore may have had the chance to have seen the Grail paintings, may have been known as 'perche-val' in France and was a brave hero associated with the Holy Lance, Goering suggests that, taken together, these facts may lie at the heart of the Grail story written by Chrétien de Troyes.

6

THE GRAIL REVIVAL

The Grail in the 18ᵗʰ and 19ᵗʰ Centuries
After the dramatic flowering of the Grail literature, which reached its peak in the 15ᵗʰ century, the interest in these stories began to decline. This was largely due to changing attitudes towards the importance of the Mass and the miracle of transubstantiation. During the Reformation the story of the Grail, which ultimately belongs outside the orthodox teachings of the Church, was viewed in very unfavourable terms. English Puritans rejected Grail literature, as did reformers in the Catholic Church. However, in the late 18ᵗʰ century, as a variety of Christian sects emerged, there was a new dissatisfaction with orthodox Christianity, both Catholic and Protestant. The new role of science in society seems also to have had an effect on religious thought. In reaction to the growing power of science, many turned back to more spiritual explanations of the meaning of life. Following a vision in 1745 Emmanuel Swedenborg, for example, rejected science in favour of 'theosophy'which broadly translates into the pursuit of understanding God. In these new social conditions, in which emerging religious groups showed a lively and active interest in spiritual and mystical matters, lay the seeds for the rediscovery of the Grail.

Another contributing factor was an increased interest in literary scholarship and the exploration of texts from the medieval period in the 18th century. Writers such as Sir Walter Scott were inspired by these works to create the genre known as the historical novel, which stimulated an appetite for subject matter relating to the Middle Ages. New editions of Malory's *Morte d'Arthur* were published at the beginning of the 19th century and proved very popular with the British public. By the middle years of Victoria's reign the Arthurian legends and the Holy Grail were once more in fashion.

However the themes of the Arthurian romances sometimes proved problematic for Victorian sensibilities. When the artist William Dyce was commissioned to decorate the Queen's Robing Room in the House of Lords he put forward the idea of using *Morte d'Arthur* as the basis for a series of frescoes. Prince Albert himself thought it a wonderful idea but the artist soon ran into problems when trying to pick scenes to paint. He felt not only that the Grail stories contained a strong Catholic element but that the adultery of Lancelot and Guinevere was at odds with respectable Victorian moral values. (Catholicism in Britain remained a particularly controversial subject at this time. It is perhaps startling to us today to remember that Catholics had only been able to worship following their own faith after an act of parliament was passed in 1829. The appointment of an English Catholic archbishop in 1850 led to riots. The effects of the Reformation were still being felt in Victorian culture.) Tennyson, whose name was to become synonymous with the Arthurian legends, was also forced to distort much of the story to make it suitable for Victorian culture. The Grail was to prove a difficult subject for him to tackle and had to be remoulded carefully so as not to offend the Church of England. But the sexual and religious elements of the Arthurian romances, sublimated or not, were to prove an irresistible combination for Victorian society. Arthuriana became something of an obsession for the Victorians and manifested itself in the photographs of Julia Margaret Cameron, the work of illustrators such as Gustave Dore and Arthur Rackham and in public and domestic decoration and furnishing.

William Blake

The visionary poet and artist William Blake was born in the city of London in 1757. His unique and highly idiosyncratic approach to his work won him few admirers in his lifetime but he has come to be recognised as one of the major figures in the history of art in the 18th and 19th centuries. His parents were religious Dissenters belonging to one of the proliferation of Christian sects that could be found in London at this time. His father was a hosier who sent his son to drawing school aged ten. Blake became an apprentice engraver aged fourteen. He was to make a living mainly through work as an engraver and painter and his poetry went largely unrecognised. Blake did not receive a formal education outside of his instruction in art but read voraciously and was influenced by the religious ideas of his parents and other religious radicals such as Swedenborg. As a child Blake had a number of striking visions. Aged between eight and ten, he claimed to have seen a tree swarming with angels in Peckham Rye. On another occasion he saw angels walking amongst a group of haymakers in the fields that used to surround the then much smaller city of London. His mother is said to have thrashed him for claiming to have met the prophet Ezekiel. It was this powerful visionary ability combined with vivid and intense biblical imagery that was to make his work so singularly compelling.

Perhaps unsurprisingly such an imaginative child was drawn to mythology and legend and, through sustained and varied reading, Blake built up an individual and unusual mythic universe of his own. His later work particularly is constructed of figures that have a mystical symbolic function and it is informed by a range of historical, religious and artistic sources. Blake read Geoffrey of Monmouth and was fascinated by the ancient history of Britain or 'Albion'. He was drawn to the mystical and the esoteric. One patron of his work, William Owen Pughe, for whom he produced a painting called 'The Ancient Britons' was said to have 'espoused the complicated mixture of Druidic allegory, Arthurian lore and comparative mythology that made so powerful an appeal to Blake himself'. (Peter Ackroyd, *Blake*, 1995, p305)

Looming large in the iconography of Blake is the figure of the bard or Druid that recurs frequently in his work. Many biographers have seen his portrayal of a lone bearded mystic usually in a wild setting such as Wales or Cornwall as being representative of Blake himself. The subject of Blake's first engraving as an apprentice was 'Joseph of Arimathea among the Rocks of Albion', 1773. He is portrayed as a lone prophet with whom the artist seems to have strongly identified.

As the founder of the first Christian church in Britain at Glastonbury where he carried the blood of Christ in the Holy Grail, he was for Blake the original architect of a spirituality that was to result in Westminster Abbey, which exerted a powerful influence over the artist. The image of the lone prophet is likely also to have been informed by the work of the antiquarian William Stukeley and in particular his book *Stonehenge: A Temple Restored to the British Druids*. The legends concerning Joseph of Arimathea's connection with Britain also relate that as a wealthy merchant he had travelled to this country previously and that Jesus Christ had accompanied him as a youth. This then forms the backdrop to one of Blake's most recognisable poems, best known today as the hymn 'Jerusalem'.

Originally written as an introductory poem to *Milton*, 1804–1810, the opening lines in particular demonstrate Blake's familiarity with these stories:

And did those feet in ancient time
Walk upon England's mountains green?
And was the holy Lamb of God
On England's pleasant pastures seen?

And did the Countenance Divine
Shine forth upon our clouded hills?
And was Jerusalem builded here
Among these dark Satanic Mills?

From an historical point of view trading links between Britain and the Mediterranean appear to have remote origins, particularly in the supply of tin from Cornwall where Joseph was said to have first landed. Whether Christ himself physically visited Britain or the story is merely a metaphor for the arrival of the Gospel is of course as much a matter for debate today as it was in Blake's lifetime. In Blake's painting *The Body of Christ Borne to the Tomb*, 1799–1800, Jesus is carried at shoulder height by a grieving group of followers. The wound in Christ's side made by the lance of Longinus is clearly visible. An old man with a flowing white beard and a staff carrying an urn appears to be leading the group away from the scene of the crucifixion. If Blake is following the biblical version of events he is Joseph of Arimathea and he may be carrying the blood of Christ in this vessel. The figure of Joseph as prophet and founding father of Albion echoes Blake's recurrent fascination with the image of the visionary either as bard, pagan Druid or Christian.

Tennyson

No other author of the Victorian era did more to popularise Arthurian subject matter than Tennyson. Through his poetry Tennyson re-cast the romances of the Middle Ages as an allegory for modern Victorian society. His handling of an established body of stories becomes informed by the values and morality of the times during which he was writing. The resurgence in interest in the art and culture of the medieval period took place in an England which had been transformed by the Industrial Revolution and in which the British Empire dominated much of the globe. A sense of looking back at a Golden Era was tempered in Tennyson's work by an underlying pessimism about the moral weakness that led to the collapse of Arthur's kingdom. For Tennyson, Arthur's rule had been a transitory period of hope and achievement undermined by the adultery of Guinevere and Lancelot and by human weakness. Merlin is undone by lust and the quest for the Holy Grail itself plays a key role in the destruction of the fellowship of the Round Table.

Born in 1809 Alfred Lord Tennyson worked on a series of poems that would collectively be known as the *Idylls of the King* (1859–1885) from his twenties up until his death in 1892. His poems were hugely successful and Queen Victoria herself asked him to continue his work on the subject. He was particularly reluctant to write about the Grail quest and continued largely through royal persuasion.

Many saw Camelot and Arthur's kingdom as an allegory for the British Empire and Tennyson may have feared that the empire too could not be sustained. The Grail itself also had symbolic links with Catholic ritual and he may have felt uncomfortable writing about this for a Church of England audience. In Tennyson's versions of the myths, Arthur does not participate in the quest and his sense of religious beliefs is bound up with an overriding sense of duty that reflects Victorian values and ideals.

Wagner

Literature and painting were not the only art forms affected by the re-kindling of interest in the Middle Ages during the 19th century. The German composer and music theorist Richard Wagner was born in 1813 and was a keen reader of medieval literature with a particular love of Arthurian mythology. He is best known for his operas such as *Der Ring des Nibelungen,* which is generally referred to as the Ring cycle. This sequence of four operas drew on Scandinavian and German mythology.

Arthurian subject matter had been the basis for an earlier work, *Tristan und Isolde,* and the story of the Holy Grail was at the heart of his final opera *Parsifal.* Wagner had read Wolfram von Eschenbach's work of the same name in 1845. The Grail inspired and obsessed Wagner throughout his life and he is reputed to have visited Rennes-le-Chateau in France because of the legends connecting the chalice cup to the town. Another popular story claims that Wagner travelled to North Wales to see the wooden Nanteos cup that had been said by some to be the actual Holy Grail. Although the opera *Parsifal* is based on Eschenbach's medieval story, it differs from his version in several respects. Most importantly the Grail takes the form of a vessel and not a stone as it is described in the original. Also the lance of Longinus, with magical healing abilities, becomes the object of the quest and the Grail temple becomes the central focus around which the opera revolves. It was first performed at Bayreuth in 1882 and Wagner himself requested that it should only be staged there. For Wagner it was a deeply spiritual work that he did not want to be altered or interfered with. In this sense the theatre itself became a kind of sacred space, a shrine to the opera itself, an idea that, incorporating as it did elements of the Eucharist, some Christians felt was blasphemous. Some critics have linked *Parsifal* with Nazi ideology, although it is difficult to reconcile this with the fact that its performance was banned in Bayreuth during the Second World War.

Pre-Raphaelites

The Pre-Raphaelites were an important and influential group of British artists of the 19th century. The founder members of what was known as the Pre-Raphaelite Brotherhood were Dante Gabriel Rossetti, John Everett Millais and William Holman Hunt. Rossetti and Millais were students together at the Royal Academy. Rossetti began his studies in 1845 and soon grew bored with the Academy tradition of working from statues and began to search for a form of artistic expression outside of the conventions of the day. Rossetti was the son of a Professor of Italian at University College who had a great passion for the poet Dante Alighieri, the medieval author of *Inferno* after whom he was named. They rejected the Academy style of the time and scorned many establishment artists of the day. Rossetti reserved particular spite for Sir Joshua, or 'Sloshua,' Reynolds as he dubbed the distinguished painter and looked instead to the influence of the medieval period, particularly religious manuscript illustration. Bright, intense colours were to be an important and recognisable part of their work. They were also particularly influenced by the art critic John Ruskin and his philosophy of observing and working directly from nature.

Rossetti used Sir Thomas Malory's *Morte d'Arthur* as the basis for a watercolour that he completed for Ruskin in 1855. He worked from the Robert Southey edition, which had been published in 1817. The main focus of the picture, entitled 'Arthur's Tomb', is the relationship between Guinevere and Lancelot and it depicts the final meeting of the lovers in an apple orchard as described by Malory. Guinevere is kneeling beside an effigy of Arthur and is holding a hand up against Lancelot who is trying to embrace her. She is wearing a nun's clothes and the tension in the picture is created by the drawing together of the three figures in the centre of the picture. On the side of Arthur's tomb are painted scenes from Camelot such as the Holy Grail floating in the air accompanied by a dove before the company of the Round Table. For Rossetti the spiritual importance of the Grail was seriously challenged by the theme of love and the triangular relationship of Arthurian legend would find echoes in his own life. He was later to embark on an affair with the wife of William Morris.

When a new edition of Tennyson's poems was published in 1855, Rossetti was approached to produce illustrations. He produced work on a number of poems with medieval themes such as the 'Lady of Shalott' and 'Sir Galahad at the Ruined Chapel'. These were translated into wood engravings and in 1859 Rossetti produced a watercolour of the Sir Galahad illustration. In this image a remote chapel in a wood is seen to come to life as Galahad approaches. He appears to be experiencing a vision of the Grail that suffuses the painting in rich colours reminiscent of illuminated manuscripts and stained glass. By using influences from the past Rossetti created a new painting style that is as much a product of the Victorian era and its influences as a real attempt to replicate the culture of the Middle Ages.

Rossetti was to find like-minded friends in the artist and designer William Morris and the painter Edward Burne-Jones. Both men were great admirers of the *Morte D'Arthur* and Burne-Jones particularly produced some exceptionally vivid and memorable work based on the theme of the Grail quest. He produced a series of tapestries entitled The Quest for the Holy Grail (1891–94) that features a particularly striking depiction of the 'Achievement of Sir Galahad'. In this image a company of angels guards the Grail. In the work of Morris and Burne-Jones the theme of the Grail provides inspiration for artistic innovation and intense creativity. It has a spirituality that seems less informed by the doctrines of a religious institution than a personal, individual sensibility.

Aubrey Beardsley

The artist and illustrator Aubrey Beardsley was to develop further the Pre-Raphaelite style and sensibility.

Born in Brighton on 21st August 1872 he was to have a brief but highly productive and influential career. Poor health was to be a defining factor in his life from an early age; he first developed tuberculosis at the age of nine. The disease recurred throughout his life and would ultimately end it at the age of just 25. His family were of middle and upper class background, but were often virtually penniless. As a child

Beardsley demonstrated prodigious artistic abilities and talents, as did his sister Mabel who went on to become an actress in adult life.

His mother also suffered from ill health and he was sent, together with his sister, to live with an aunt at the age of twelve. Whilst at boarding school he demonstrated and experimented with his abilities as an artist by drawing satirical portraits of his teachers. Beardsley's professional work as an illustrator was often to combine the grotesque with the shocking and controversial, and sometimes even led to his work being described as pornographic. His first job was working as an insurance clerk in a London office, which he began in 1889. Although Beardsley had no real interest in the post it offered him the chance to continue his interest in caricature, using his fellow workers as subject matter. He drew continually whilst in the office, inspired by the variety of people who visited the firm. His new appointment also provided him with the opportunity to visit London's galleries and museums and, perhaps most importantly, its bookshops.

Beardsley developed a keen interest in Italian art and culture and was particularly drawn to the medieval period. He also became fascinated by the work of Dante Gabriel Rossetti who had died in 1882. His interest in Rossetti extended to the other Pre-Raphaelite artists and also prompted him to read the poetry of Dante Alighieri.

Beardsley became increasingly convinced that he should pursue a career in art and had a few small successes in having poetry and sketches published in a number of periodicals of the day. However, impatient to leave his job as a clerk he made an unannounced visit to the studio of Edward Burne-Jones with his sister in an attempt to gain approval and advice on an artistic career from the famous painter. Initially they were turned away by a servant, but the artist himself rushed out to meet them, apparently captivated by Mabel's vivid red hair. After viewing his portfolio of work Burne-Jones is reputed to have said, 'I seldom or never advise anyone to take up art as a profession, but in your case I can do nothing else' (Matthew Sturgis, *Aubrey Beardsley*, p73).

This was to prove a pivotal moment in the life and career of Beardsley who felt massively encouraged by the words of his artistic hero. Burne-Jones recommended that he take night classes at the Westminster School of Art, which allowed Beardsley to combine the dull but necessary office work with the development of a new artistic career.

In 1892 he was introduced to the publisher J. M. Dent through the bookseller Frederick Evans. Evans was aware that one of Dent's next major projects was to be an illustrated partwork publication of Sir Thomas Malory's *Morte d'Arthur*. Dent was building a reputation for producing well-designed editions of classic works that were produced cheaply with a new photomechanical process. They were influenced by William Morris's Kelmscott Press but were far less expensive and time-consuming to produce. Evans recommended the young artist to the publisher and showed him some of his work, which was displayed in his bookshop. In particular Dent wanted illustrations in the style of Burne-Jones and recognised this element in Beardsley's work. Initially taken aback by the scale of the project Beardsley was nonetheless thrilled at the prospect of illustrating a work he knew and loved and undertaking his first major commission as an illustrator. He agreed to produce a sample of work based on the story and produced an illustration depicting 'The Achieving of the Sangreal'. The picture combines Italian influences with pictorial ideas drawn from the Japanese woodcuts which had become increasingly popular in artistic circles of the time. Dent, highly impressed by the illustration, offered Beardsley the commission. The work was issued in 12 parts and at a later date as a complete work and featured over 300 illustrations of varying function and format. Such an extensive and well-paid commission allowed Beardsley to fulfil his personal quest of becoming a professional artist and there is a happy irony that it should be through his drawing of the achievement of the Grail. Although other work produced for the book sometimes strayed into the macabre and at times parodied the Arthurian romance, his illustration of the Grail has a spiritual and respectful quality.

7

A MODERN OBSESSION

The Grail in the 20th Century

The symbolic flexibility of the Grail has never been more apparent than in the 20th century. Its mirror-like qualities have reflected the major concerns of a western world shaped by industrialisation and the traumas of war and the decline of Christianity.

In the aftershock of Darwin's theories regarding evolution and the development of man, biblical certainties increasingly gave way to a tidal wave of questioning and the rise of science as the new and defining authority in society. It is in this context that the Grail continued to provide inspiration to artists and thinkers who found elements in the myth that were relevant to the problems of 20th century life. Perhaps the theme connected to the Grail that has had most resonance in the 20th century has been the concept of the wasteland. In the shattered, hellish landscape of the First World War a new wasteland emerged created by a new mechanistic violence. The negative associations of the Grail predominate in responses to wars fought by the means of mass production. Interestingly, the figure of Galahad was very popular in war memorials and had been since the Victorian era. But the Catholic traditions of the mass that he had previously represented were to become secularised as he came to define an ideal of the young warrior.

The darker, more destructive aspects of the quest and the Grail legends, such as obsessiveness, self-destruction and madness, have also been highlighted in the context of 20th century history. Adolf Hitler's love of the composer Wagner was to result in the appropriation and manipulation of the Grail myth for the dark and evil ends of the Nazi party.

Anthropologists and writers such as Jessie Weston and the psychologist Carl Jung undertook a closer examination of the detectable themes and influences within the Grail tradition. Weston's book *From Ritual to Romance* (1920) examined the pre-Christian aspects of the Grail and succeeded in unleashing a tidal wave of speculation about its origins, ranging from the plausible to the far-fetched. With the decline of orthodox Christianity there has been a rise in New Age beliefs, which have focused on the pagan elements in the Grail legends. The re-establishment of Glastonbury as a major spiritual centre also served to re-awaken interest in the Grail. In 1906 a small blue glass bowl was found in the Bride's Well at Glastonbury and it was claimed to be the Grail itself. Conspiracy theories and ideas about concealed traditions and alternative histories, which have expanded generally within Western society, have also attached themselves to the Grail. The theories of Michael Baigent, Richard Leigh and Henry Lincoln and their book *The Holy Blood and the Holy Grail*, which have been discussed earlier, are typical of this trend.

Interest in Arthurian subjects has remained high and it is fascinating to observe the extent to which names and ideas related to this subject have become part of what Jung referred to as the 'collective unconscious'. During John F. Kennedy's presidency the White House became known as Camelot and, following his assassination on November 22, 1963, it came to represent a lost golden age of opportunity in American politics. The president and his wife Jackie had enjoyed listening to the soundtrack of the musical *Camelot* and he had read the stories of the Round Table as a child. Journalists were to link his aspirational presidency with the ideals of Camelot and his death was to be one of the great traumas in the history of modern America.

Grail references are to be found in a host of secular and irreverent contexts from the Elvis Presley film *Kid Galahad* to the teenage wasteland of the classic Who song, 'Baba O'Riley'. Perhaps most tellingly the context in which the Holy Grail seems most commonly to occur in modern times is that of the world of science. It is often used to describe an ultimate scientific goal or achievement. No doubt this reflects the fact that science has come to dominate the mysterious and profound areas in the life of individuals and society that religion used to occupy.

T. S. Eliot

The Grail legend is one of the key influences on T. S. Eliot's poetic masterpiece, *The Waste Land*. Written in 1922 it is considered by many to be amongst the most important poems of the 20th century. Perhaps ironically the poem is less concerned with the Grail itself and focuses more on the lack of spirituality in contemporary society. Eliot's modernist poem broke with previous stylistic conventions and arguably resembles more closely cinematic and artistic techniques such as montage. The poem is formed from an impressive array of literary, historical and mythological references and the story of the Grail provides just one of the elements from which Eliot creates his work. In particular *The Waste Land* incorporates the figure of the wounded Fisher King and his kingdom that has been laid waste following his injury.

In the notes to the poem Eliot himself acknowledged the influence of Jessie Weston's *From Ritual to Romance* and its exploration of ancient fertility and vegetation rites particularly in relation to the Grail stories. The poem was written during a particularly difficult period in the poet's life when he was suffering ill health and his own marriage was faltering. It underwent several stages of revision and the poet Ezra Pound played an important part in helping Eliot structure and edit the poem.

Written in the immediate aftermath of the First World War the poem is very much a product of its times, expressing the despair and sense of chaotic disorder which dominated much of Europe in the early part of the 20th century. Some have argued that the collapse of the old social orders is the cause of much of the poem's sense of anxiety and hopelessness. Eliot, by his own admission, was a Conservative and Royalist and the disappearance of a traditional, hierarchical way of life in post-First World War Europe is reflected in many of the characters in the poem.The Fisher King is portrayed in the contemporary barren urban wasteland setting of the city of London as Eliot describes him,

> '. . . fishing in the dull canal
> On a winter evening round behind the gashouse . . . '
> (*The Waste Land* Part Three: The Fire Sermon, Line 189)

Eliot also describes a harrowing journey to the Grail chapel by a questing knight who travels through a waterless desert landscape, suffering from thirst and fatigue. On finding the ruined chapel a storm breaks and the flash of lightning brings the life-renewing force of rain. This allusion to the release of water echoes the return of water to the lands of the Fisher King.

However, in the final part of the poem the King seems still to be suffering from a kind of powerless inertia as he describes himself,

> 'Fishing, with the arid plain behind me
> Shall I at least put my lands in order?'
> (*The Waste Land* Part Five: What the Thunder Said, Line 424)

For Eliot the increasingly secular society of the early part of the 20th century was becoming more sterile, vacuous and culturally arid. Sexual relationships are portrayed as empty and meaningless and the lost fertility of the Fisher King becomes particularly emblematic of this. Occult interests such as Tarot readings replace spirituality and the new religion of consumerism and materialism has overtaken people. The industrialisation of society has also affected the lives of individuals, who, by performing mechanistic, repetitive actions, are transformed into a kind of 'human engine'. However, the poem offers a glimpse of hope in its final section where the language struggles to unite the spirituality of both the Eastern and Western religious traditions.

Jung

The Grail was to offer a rich tradition of symbolism to the Swiss psychologist and thinker Carl Jung (1875– 1961). He had been fascinated by the stories from childhood when he first read them in his father's library. It was a myth that he was to come to believe was amongst the most important in Western civilisation. Jung was initially deeply influenced by the work of Freud with whom he developed a close friendship and who was originally a mentor to him. However, Jung eventually grew to disagree with many of Freud's basic theories and developed ideas of his own about human psychology. He was to be a hugely influential psychologist, theorist and thinker and many of the terms and concepts he coined and defined have become part of our everyday language and outlook.

Whilst exploring the idea of the conscious and unconscious mind of the individual, Jung put forward the argument that there also existed a collective unconscious, which was shared by the whole of humanity. The collective unconscious for Jung consisted of a shared pool of symbolism, which was very often expressed in the form of religions, myths and legends. With this in mind he undertook a detailed study of a number of world religions and myths and found what he felt was a striking number of parallels between them. He observed that very often they consisted of stories based around a recognisable series of figures, which he described as archetypes. These archetypal figures were common to all cultures and described a typical human experience.

Although Jung had a particular interest and fondness for the Arthurian stories and the Grail myths, it was to become a special area of study for his wife Emma who was researching a book on the subject before her death. Co-written with Marie-Louise Von Franz, it was published posthumously as *The Grail Legend*. They examine the Grail legend in Jungian terms and explore its Celtic origins as cauldron of plenty and its transformation into a Christian artefact.

Here the Grail develops redemptive qualities and represents a spiritual search for a higher understanding. The characters from the story are shown to be basic archetypes. Perceval is described as the fool embarking on a journey and the hermit Gornemanz, who advises and encourages him, is the 'wise old man' who figures in so many fairy tales and legends. This analysis of the story argues that Perceval is embarking on both an inner and outer journey and that he is undergoing what Carl Jung called the process of 'individuation' or self-development, and seeking the ultimate integration of all the elements of the ego, self and psyche. Perhaps most importantly the Jungian analysis of the Grail legend stresses that it is still of relevance and importance to people today and, through it, they can explore both everyday issues and the broader Western backdrop of Christian thought and culture.

Jung was particularly interested in alchemy and the concept of transforming base metals into gold. The alchemical elements that occur in some of the Grail texts (such as the Grail in the form of a stone in Wolfram Von Eschenbach's version) led him to speculate that the Grail knight is undergoing just such a transformative experience himself.

Carl Jung travelled widely, exploring different cultures and ideas, and travelled to Britain on several occasions with his wife Emma to visit sites linked to the Grail such as Glastonbury and locations in Cornwall. Jung had wide-ranging interests that took in the occult, gnosticism and the paranormal and he believed that all these areas offered insights into the human psyche. The language and interpretation of dreams also played a major part in the development of his approach to psychology. From childhood he paid particular attention to his own dreams, sometimes acting as his own analyst. Whilst travelling in India Jung had an extremely vivid dream about the Holy Grail that he felt was one of the most powerful he had in his entire life. In it he was trying to reach the Grail which was being kept on an island off the coast of England and which was divided in two by a body of water. His final memory of the dream was the decision to swim across the water to reach the Grail. Jung concluded that the Grail was a symbol of enlightenment and that it held a key place in the Western psyche as an illustration of an ultimate goal. He was to continue to explore his relationship with Christianity and the Grail in his work and studies throughout his life.

Tolkien

J. R. R. Tolkien is widely acknowledged as one of the most popular authors of the last century. His epic fantasy trilogy *The Lord of the Rings* is regularly voted the best book of all time in polls and surveys although his works seem to have as many critics as admirers. A respected Oxford professor specialising in philology or the study of ancient languages, his great passion for mythology and literature was to shape his own imaginary sagas. Born in 1892 in Bloemfontein, South Africa, he spent his childhood in the West Midlands near Birmingham in England. The effects of urbanisation and industrialisation in this area were to affect Tolkien profoundly as he watched the rural England of his childhood memories being swallowed up by the expansion of the city.

The horrors of the First World War were also to influence his writing as he spent four months fighting in the trenches before being sent home suffering from 'trench fever', a strain of typhoid. Many of his contemporaries were less fortunate and there are strong echoes of their suffering in *The Lord of the Rings*, which was published in three volumes in 1954 and 1955. Tolkien became a Professor at Oxford University and was enthralled by early European history and literature. He collaborated on a translation of the medieval romance of *Gawain and the Green Knight* in 1925 with E. V. Gordon. However, although he had a wide knowledge of the Arthurian tales, he regarded them as being primarily French in origin. His particular interest lay in Anglo-Saxon culture, which he felt had been suppressed by the invading Normans, leaving England without a truly great mythology of its own. It was the desire to produce a great fictional saga that was to culminate in *The Lord of the Rings*. Nonetheless there are many undeniable parallels between the Arthurian romances and his fantasy trilogy, which is underpinned by the central theme of quest. Like the Grail romances the quest which is undertaken is perilous and difficult and ultimately can only be achieved by one special individual. But where the Grail is a beneficent, healing, heavenly talisman, the ring of power, which Frodo the hobbit bears, is powerful, corrupting and malevolent. His quest is to destroy the ring in the fires of Mount Doom where it was created by the evil Lord Sauron. Echoes of the Grail romances still emerge in this context, as the ultimate destination of the questers in both instances is an other-worldly mountain. The Arthurian influence is also pronounced in the titles of two of the three books. *The Fellowship of the Ring* echoes the equality and sense of hope of the fellowship of the Round Table and *The Return of the King* evokes the legend of Arthur's promised resurrection. Like Arthur, the king in question, Aragorn, son of Arathorn, is an heir to a kingdom who is revealed to his people by a mysterious wizard, Gandalf the Grey. He most obviously resembles the wizard Merlin and also acts as advisor, magician and prophet.

Aragorn must pursue a personal Grail in recovering his kingship and in the absence of a rightful sovereign the land is laid waste by a marauding army of Orcs. Like Eliot, Tolkien saw the industrial age of machines as a destructive and negative force most powerfully expressed in the brutality and inhumanity of modern warfare. The forces of the Dark Lord Sauron are linked with violent technologies and the destruction of the natural world whose power emanates from the ring. It has the power only to create a wasteland, not to heal it. As the fellowship of the Round Table is effectively destroyed by the Grail quest, the fellowship of the Ring is ultimately torn apart by the journey to destroy the ring.

Many have commented on the obvious parallels between Sauron and Adolf Hitler and the destructive conflict of World War Two. Tolkien drew on many sources and ideas for his fully realised vision of the world he called Middle-Earth. Its timeless battle between the forces of good and evil linked with his natural storytelling abilities explain much of the huge popularity of the books. To find that it is underpinned by elements drawn from the Grail legends serves to emphasise their own continuing potency.

T. H. White

One of the most popular 20th century re-tellings of the Arthurian legends was written by the author T.H.White (1906–1964). Beginning with *The Sword in the Stone* in 1939, White charts the life of King Arthur from a small boy, when he is comically known as 'Wart', to the foundation of Camelot and then his final departure to Avalon. It was followed by *The Witch in the Wood* (1939), *The Ill-made Knight* (1940), *Candle in the Wind* (1958) and the posthumous publication of *The Book of Merlyn* (1977). The whole series, apart from *The Book of Merlyn*, appeared as a single volume entitled *The Once and Future King* in 1958. Based on Malory's *Morte d'Arthur*, it

approaches the subject matter from a distinctly contemporary
point of view and is particularly memorable for its use of
humour. White incorporated humour into his work as a device
to make the subject matter more accessible to a modern audience. He also adds reference points that derive from historical
periods that are later than the medieval context in which he sets
the stories. Once again the intention is to provide the reader
with ideas and concepts with which they will be familiar, in an
attempt to overcome the sense of distance from the past, and
also to highlight parallels with the present.

White explored a number of themes through the Arthurian
stories that have relevance to modern society such as leader-
ship, war, power, love and religion. The Grail quest is seen
very much with a sceptical, semi-cynical 20th century eye and
the focus is on its divisive and destructive qualities. Galahad,
in particular, is depicted as cold and aloof, a virgin knight
who lacks compassion and empathy, embodying that strain
of Christian faith which has disconnected itself from earthly
concerns to concentrate instead on heavenly perfection.
Percivale receives a warmer, more sympathetic treatment as
an innocent fool who is just as worthy to achieve the Grail as
Galahad. When Percivale is criticised by another knight for
his clumsy unsuitability to find the Grail, Arthur retorts, 'If
God is merciful, I don't see why He shouldn't allow people
to stumble into heaven, just as well as climb there'. (T. H.
White, *The Once and Future King*, HarperCollins, 1996
edition, p490.)

White often plays down the more magical elements of the
Quest saying, 'If you want to read about the beginning of
the Quest for the Grail . . . and of the last supper at court, when
the thunder came and the sunbeam and the covered vessel and
the sweet smell through the Great Hall . . . you must seek them
in Malory. That way of telling the story can only be done once.'
(T. H. White, *The Once and Future King*, HarperCollins, 1996
edition, p471.) In showing respect and admiration for Malory,
White seems also to acknowledge the increasingly secular and

cynical nature of the 20th century and his over-riding theme is the loss of faith in a mechanistic age dominated by science. The quest ends not in a scene of religious rapture or spiritual fulfilment but with the ragged and exhausted figure of Lancelot returning to Camelot with the news that the Grail had been found by Galahad, Percivale and Bors.

They had then travelled with it to Sarras in Babylon. The Grail will not return to Camelot and Bors will be the only knight to return of the three.

Joseph Campbell

Following the work of Jung, the writer and mythographer Joseph Campbell made an exhaustive study of the Grail legends. Born in 1904, Campbell had a childhood fascination with the culture of American Indians and rapidly developed an interest in many different world cultures and myths. He studied medieval literature at university and was particularly interested in the Arthurian stories. Campbell's wide-ranging studies and examination of world myths led to the writing of *The Hero with a Thousand Faces*, published in 1949. In this work Campbell makes the suggestion that there is a universal 'monomyth', a phrase he took from James Joyce, that follows a basic pattern and is common to all cultures. He applies this argument to the Grail romances and makes similar suggestions to Jung that Parsival and other characters within the tales are universal archetypes. He also put forward the idea that these tales follow a 'mythic cycle' that unfolds in several distinct stages which he names and describes. Campbell argues that these mythic cycles not only have value for individuals as metaphors for life experiences but that they extend further to the cultures that the individuals live within.

In *The Masks of God: Creative Mythology*, published in 1968, he makes a particularly close study of the roots of the Grail legends. Through comparative studies of world religions and legends. Campbell asserts that the Grail has its basis in much earlier mystery cults which were carried from the Mediterranean countries into Europe by the Romans. The examples he suggests include Orphic, Mithraic, Gnostic, and Manichean traditions. Campbell also saw parallels between wheel imagery in Hindu legends and the revolving castles of Celtic Arthurian stories. In both sets of stories a ritual question needs to be asked and the symbolism of the rotating wheel is suggestive of the cycle of life and death. Campbell's theories on world myth have influenced many artists and *The Hero With A Thousand Faces* was to shape George Lucas's screenplay for the 1977 science fiction film classic *Star Wars*.

Hitler and the Nazis

Although some claims that have linked Hitler with the Grail have been wildly exaggerated, they have some basis in truth. Most importantly the work of Wagner provided inspiration to Hitler and the emergent National Socialism movement in proclaiming a new social and racial elite. Most vividly, indeed luridly, Hitler is quoted as having spoken of a 'brotherhood of Templars around the Grail of pure blood' (Richard Barber, *The Holy Grail*, p317). The imagery of the work of Richard Wagner was used to proclaim the new nationalistic fervour and this has come to taint, unfairly, the work of the composer. However, it is undeniable that Hitler was moved and inspired by the opera *Parsifal* and it was a work that exerted a powerful influence on his life and thought.

The Nazis did attempt to prove that the Aryan peoples were the first civilisation through the exploration of pre-history and archaeological excavations. The primary concern of such work was to identify and restore an alleged ancient German religion and many of the results of this were distorted to fit the required propaganda model. A German writer called Otto Rahn developed a disturbing Nazi hypothesis concerning the Cathars and the Grail. In *The Courtiers of Lucifer* written in 1937 he claimed that the Cathars were Aryans who venerated the Grail as a symbol of Lucifer. Rahn argued that Christianity was a Jewish religion designed to benefit the Jews. This bizarre distortion of history to suit propaganda purposes also resulted in the development of a series of contentious theories and stories connecting the Grail to the Nazis.

8

THE CINEMA OF THE GRAIL

Representations in Film

There have been many films based on Arthurian mythology and the Grail Quest. Some, such as *Perceval le Gallois* (1978) by Eric Rohmer, have stuck closely to the original stories (in Rohmer's case the work of Chrétien de Troyes) but others have re-interpreted the symbolism of the Grail. A striking example is John Boorman's *Excalibur* (1981), which explores some of its underlying pre-Christian themes.

Director Terry Gilliam, part of the Monty Python team that irreverently poked fun at the legends, was also drawn back to the subject for *The Fisher King* starring Robin Williams in 1991. Even whilst de-bunking the myth Gilliam, who co-directed the Monty Python film, seemed to have an unabashed love for the inherent beauty and poetry of the stories.

The musical *Camelot* was translated to film, with Richard Harris in the role of Arthur. This has been one of the best-known and popular screen versions of the story, which as explored in the previous chapter came to have an added resonance with the assassination of John F. Kennedy. It has also provided something of a storytelling blueprint for the films of George Lucas and Steven Spielberg. With the recent adaptation of the *Lord of the Rings,* aspects of the Grail mythology are again found at the heart of popular entertainment. Like John Boorman's *Excalibur,* these films have a strong underlying environmental theme. Interestingly, *King Arthur,* released in 2004, has attempted to portray a historically accurate version of the legend set in post-Roman Britain and does not include the Grail, reflecting its status as a later addition to the canon. The sheer number of films that have either directly explored Arthurian legends, or been influenced by them, arguably supports Carl Jung's idea that Grail mythology provides some of the most important archetypal stories in Western culture.

George Lucas

The Grail tradition took on space age trappings with the George Lucas fantasy epic *Star Wars* (1977). It was conceived as a futuristic adventure story but a clue to its origins and inspirations is revealed ironically by the fact that it is set in the remote past, 'a long time ago, in a galaxy far, far away ...' Behind the technology of spaceships and lasers lies a narrative that has clear parallels with Arthurian legend. Although the influences on Star Wars are many, it is fundamentally a film about the Sacred Quest.

Tellingly, many have described *Star Wars* as a space opera, recalling the works of Richard Wagner such as *Parsifal* and the *Ring* cycle. The mythological and fantasy elements of Wagner find echoes in *Star Wars* and its suitably rousing soundtrack score by composer John Williams. Director George Lucas, a hugely knowledgeable fan of cinema, pays homage to a number of sources ranging from the films of Akira Kurosawa, the Flash Gordon serials of the 1930s, World War Two epics such as the *Dam Busters* to the Western genre. Special effects legend Ray Harryhausen was also an influence on Lucas and his contemporaries and inspired in them a keen interest in ancient history and mythology that would emerge in their own work. Lucas was also familiar with the theories of anthropologist Joseph Campbell and particularly his book, *The Hero with a Thousand*

Faces (1949) in which Campbell postulated the existence of a universal monomyth. Campbell had been referring to the undeniable similarities that exist between the myths and legends of people from different countries and cultures. Arguably, Lucas took this idea to its logical conclusion by creating a new mythology set on other planets in another galaxy.

It is interesting to note the similarities between Campbell's 'map' of the monomyth and the structure of the *Star Wars* saga and in particular its link to the Arthurian Grail tradition. In addition to this narrative outline many legends appear to have common mythic elements. The three main stages in the Adventure of the Hero are described as Departure, Initiation and Return. In the first stage of Departure the Hero commonly experiences a Call to Adventure. For the central protagonist of *Star Wars*, Luke Skywalker, his Call to Adventure is the arrival of the droids R2 D2 and C3 PO on his home world, the desert planet of Tatooine. In particular R2 D2 plays the role of the herald, bringing with him a plea for help in the form of a hologram from the captured Princess Leia. In many versions of the Grail story Perceval has grown up in a remote forest or, in one instance, in the wilderness of Snowdonia, far from the court of Camelot. One day he sees a group of knights and decides to follow them back to court and become a knight himself.

Luke is advised by Obi Wan Kenobi, a Jedi knight who acts as a wise guide to him and who hands him a magical talisman, the lightsabre that belonged to Luke's father. Obi Wan can be seen to fulfil the role of Merlin who has set the sword in the stone and is instrumental in Arthur gaining the magic sword Excalibur. The order of the Jedi to which Obi Wan belongs recalls the fellowship of the round table and its pledges to uphold the king's law and be both just and fair. Arthur proves his right to kingship by drawing the sword and only the appointed Grail champion is able to sit in the 'siege perilous', a magical seat at the round table that swallows up those unworthy to sit in it. So Luke discovers that he has the ability to use the force, a mystical universal energy, and embarks on a quest to rescue Princess Leia and to become a Jedi knight.

During the stage of Initiation, Luke travels to the planet Dagobah in the *Empire Strikes Back* (1980) where he is trained by Jedi master Yoda, who is himself an embodiment of the figure of the oracle. Perceval travels through dark forests in pursuit of the Grail and is advised by a religious hermit.

Luke has to confront his inner demons in a sacred grove and to realise that Darth Vader is his father. In the Grail stories Galahad is the son of Lancelot who cannot achieve the Grail because of his adulterous love for Guinevere. Both Luke and Galahad reach reconciliation with their fathers upon the completion of their quests. Luke becomes a Jedi and resists the Evil Emperor, who is ultimately destroyed, and Galahad finds the Holy Grail.

In some respects Luke combines aspects of the personalities of both Perceval and Galahad. At first, he seems to have the naivety of Perceval and appears to fit the role of the fool who goes on to prove his worth. But he is also brave and like Galahad pursues a spiritual path of purity. The *Star Wars* films broke new ground in terms of special effects and technical cinematic invention, pushing back the boundaries of what was possible in the medium of film. Stunning imagery in conjunction with a mythology that appeared to tap deep into the universal psyche made the *Star Wars* films globally popular and George Lucas into a multi-millionaire.

Steven Spielberg

The hero's quest was also to form the basis for *Indiana Jones and the Last Crusade* (1989). Directed by Steven Spielberg and based on a story by George Lucas, it was the third film in the Indiana Jones trilogy. Once again Lucas drew inspiration from the Arthurian legends, this time having Indiana Jones (Harrison Ford) and his father (Sean Connery) in pursuit of the Holy Grail itself. Spielberg like Lucas was also strongly drawn to the subject. Producer Lawrence Kasdan has commented that the story of the Grail is 'hugely powerful to Steven, who sees most of his movies that way' (John Baxter, *George Lucas:A Biography*, p374). In many ways the film rests on popular but unconfirmed theories about the Grail and develops its legendary qualities to fit the mould of a Hollywood blockbuster. Indiana Jones and his father become involved in a race to find the Grail with the Nazis who are seeking it for the Führer. Their quest finally leads them to Petra in Jordan where they find the Grail in the possession of a mysterious elderly knight. In Spielberg and Lucas's interpretation of the powers of the Grail, it can confer eternal life on anyone who drinks from it. Thus the Grail guardian, who appears to have been modelled on the Knights Templar, is in fact hundreds of years old. He recognises in Indiana Jones Junior a worthy successor for the role of Grail keeper when he passes a test to select the true Grail from amongst a collection of chalice cups and vessels. Spielberg has Ford select the most ordinary clay cup, the 'cup of a carpenter', emphasising purity and humility over the ostentatious and worldly Grail chosen by businessman Donovan (Julian Glover) who represents the Nazis. Donovan is aged prematurely and killed by the false Grail whilst Jones is able to use the true Grail to heal his father. In this Grail story, the chalice cannot be carried outside of the caves in which it is kept and when the Nazis try to remove it the caves fall down around them.

Indiana Jones and the Last Crusade revels in the more fanciful and exotic theories connected with the Grail whilst using the themes of quest and healing to form the narrative of the film. In creating another global box office success, Lucas and Spielberg once again put ancient themes into the heart of mainstream cinema.

John Boorman
Excalibur, directed by John Boorman, is probably the best-known film based on the Arthurian legends. Released in 1981 it is a lavish and stirring representation of Arthur and the Grail

quest, which is based on the work of Sir Thomas Malory. It immediately drew criticisms in terms of its historical accuracy, often for example mixing armour and weapons from different periods. However, Boorman's intention was to depict a mythic truth rather than to pursue historical accuracy and that liberates the film to draw on a wide variety of sources and makes it a visually rich and eloquent film. Arguably, the film follows in the tradition of up-dating the story of Arthur as Malory himself did. The theories of Carl Jung were to be a major influence on the film and it contains many actual dream sequences and dream-like fantasies. Although visually the look of the film incorporates costume and armour from the late medieval period, its themes can be traced to the Celtic and Pre-Celtic periods. The film, according to Boorman, owes a considerable debt to Jessie Weston's *From Ritual to Romance* and draws a particularly vivid link between the health and vitality of the land and King Arthur.

The characterisation of Merlin in *Excalibur* proved particularly contentious. Actor Nicol Williamson plays him as part mystic Seer and part Holy Fool. This comedic representation of the great wizard confused many on its initial release. However, Boorman had been influenced by Jung's theories about archetypal figures and particularly the role of the magician as trickster. Viewed in this light the unusual playing of Merlin makes a great deal more sense. He is mysterious and powerful but eccentric and fallible, shrewd and experienced yet capable of humour and wryly observant of the short-comings of men.

Perhaps more importantly Boorman envisaged the Arthurian cycle as being a metaphor for the history of humanity. Arthur's father Uther Pendragon, although violent and primal, has a strong connection with the power of nature through the magic of Merlin, which symbolises the remote past. Arthur takes the sword of power from his father and creates Camelot where gradually order and social control develop and mankind loses its link with nature. This reflects the sense of separation between mankind and nature that has occurred in modern society. In *Excalibur*, the affair of Guinevere and Lancelot results in the wounding of Arthur. He plunges Excalibur between the two sleeping lovers into the land and symbolically loses his power. Boorman takes the figure of the wounded Fisher King and merges him with Arthur, a bold narrative device that both confuses and simplifies the legend. The Grail must be found in order to heal Arthur and to make the land flower again. For Boorman the Grail is a Jungian symbol of feminine completeness, a means to restore a lost link with the earth. In this sense the film explores a pagan spirituality with a strong emphasis on the connection between man and nature. Christianity is represented during the wedding of Arthur and Guinevere but the Grail is not explicitly stated to be a Christian symbol. Although it is represented as a chalice cup, it seems to have more in common with the Celtic cauldrons of re-birth.

Like earlier versions of the tale, the quest for the Grail is completed by Perceval, not Galahad, and his journey has features that are reminiscent of older, pagan traditions. Perceval has his first vision of the Grail during a near-death experience when the enchantress Morgana hangs him from a tree. This recalls the story of Odin hanging from the world tree Ygdrassil in order to gain knowledge and insight. However, he fails to answer the ritual questions, 'What is the secret of the Grail? Whom does it serve?' His second vision occurs whilst drowning in a river, again recalling a druidic near-death ritual. He symbolically escapes from his armour, which has become rusted and damaged and approaches the Grail castle semi-naked. He answers the question that the land and the king are one, and that the Grail serves the king, resulting in the healing of Arthur. The Grail serves a redemptive and rejuvenating function as Perceval experiences a re-birth along with the king and the land.

Location shooting for *Excalibur* took place in Ireland and the film overall has a strong Irish influence. This has been criticised by some but as we have seen the intermingling of

Irish, Welsh and Breton influences has a basis in the oral story-telling traditions of the past. Once again this creates a mythically true reality even if it does not slavishly follow the work of Malory.

Boorman took particular trouble to film many of the exterior scenes in the ancient oak forests that have survived in Ireland. This was intended to demonstrate the ancient roots of the tale and its pre-historic elements. In the early stages of Arthur's kingship the forests are lit with a luminous green light giving a heightened sense of magic and natural vitality. In his autobiography Boorman recalled that 'we shone emerald light at the oaks and on to the swords and armour, to enhance the mystical sense of the forest as a palpable living thing' (John Boorman, *Adventures of a Suburban Boy*, p241).

Music was another powerful component in dramatising the link between the land and the king and his healing by the Grail. Richard Wagner's *Prelude to Parsifal* and *Prelude to Tristan and Isolde* appear on the soundtrack. However, it is *O Fortuna* from Carl Orff's musical adaptation of the *Carmina Burana* that remains the most memorable piece of music from the film, matched as it is to images of Arthur and his knights riding through orchards of trees in full bloom. Both thrilling and celebratory, these scenes underscore Boorman's obsession with humanity's connection with nature. It is perhaps not surprising that a film made in the late 1970s, during a period when concern over the damage being done to the environment was growing, should focus so closely on the inter-relationship between people and the planet. In this context the Grail comes to symbolise a means of healing this great damaging rift.

Monty Python

A far more irreverent version of the Grail legend was made by the Monty Python team in 1975. The first major film to be made by the Pythons chose the medieval subject matter as the basis for what is essentially a series of sketches. *Monty Python and the Holy Grail* is a curious mixture of quirky oddball comedy and surprisingly beautiful, poetic imagery which, whilst mocking the Arthurian myth, seems strangely in thrall to it.

On closer examination the primary target for satire would seem to be the romantic Victorian treatment of the story, typified by the work of Tennyson and the Pre-Raphaelites. Monty Python's film and television work often poked fun at Victorian ideals and values, particularly through the animated work of Terry Gilliam. Imagery drawn from Victorian sources is ridiculed and mocked and religious and social pomposity undermined.

God is depicted as an archaic illustration of a bearded man in the sky who appears before Arthur and his knights. Bad-tempered and crotchety he sets the knights of the Round Table a 'task to make them an example in these dark times'. The Grail appears in its most recognisable form as a chalice cup, depicted like a piece of Victorian theatrical scenery amongst clouds which creak clumsily shut once the task has been set.

Once again the Grail appears in a social and artistic context that can be regarded as groundbreaking and innovative. The Monty Python team had created a style of comedy which some found hilarious but others baffling and nonsensical. The aura of controversy that accompanied the Pythons led to difficulties in finding suitable locations for filming in Scotland. After initially agreeing to several sites for filming, the Department of the Environment for Scotland retracted permission for the use of various castles. They issued a statement saying that they were concerned that the castles might be used in ways that were 'inconsistent with the dignity of the fabric of the building'. Michael Palin pointed out the irony of this statement in the context of the history of the military use of a castle. 'Is it any more dignified', he asked, 'to pour boiling oil on someone's head from a battlement than to allow the filming of some light comedy?' The misrepresentation of history can be seen as one of the film's key motifs. They contrast the archaic romantic language attributed to the medieval period with the bleak, muddy, dirty reality of most people's lives to create a sometimes disturbing but comic effect. In one scene Eric Idle plays a man who collects the dead of a village and heaps them in a cart. The cheapness of human life and human mortality becomes a source for black comedy when John Cleese tries to get rid of a relative who 'isn't quite dead'. On seeing King Arthur pass by, a peasant played by Eric Idle concludes that he must be a king because, 'he hasn't got shit all over him'.

Monty Python and the Holy Grail spoofs a variety of subject matter from the films of Ingmar Bergman to the budget of the film itself. Because the production cannot stretch to horses, King Arthur (Graham Chapman) is accompanied by a servant, Patsy, who knocks together two coconut halves to create the sound of horses' hooves. (Ironically, the film was made fairly cheaply at around £200,000 and went on to make a large sum of money at the box office.) Like T.H. White the characters use modern speech and reference points but taken to a more jarring and striking extreme. Michael Palin plays a peasant who argues in Marxist terminology with King Arthur and who shouts out when Arthur grabs his arm, 'There, do you see the violence inherent in the system!' Such devices make us laugh but also raise questions about our interpretation of history.

'Sir Galahad the Chaste', as played by Palin, finds himself trapped in Castle Anthrax by a bevy of nymphomaniac Grail maidens. Galahad has had a vision of the Grail floating above the castle and arrives exhausted and dishevelled seeking to fulfil his quest. He is reluctantly 'rescued' by Sir Lancelot (John Cleese) so that he can retain his chaste title. Some have found this scene to have dated in a more politically correct society but the mocking of Galahad's perfect asexual image could be seen as an attack on the prurience and repressive values of Victorian and Christian Puritanism.

The Monty Python team went further in exposing the mechanics of film making and revealing the artificiality of what the audience is watching by interposing a modern day historian making a documentary about King Arthur who is himself killed by one of the knights. Ultimately the quest for the Grail fails because the entire cast is arrested when a police van turns up at the end of the film just prior to a major battle. This is a startling device that highlights the extent to which the audience has been drawn in by the ridiculous but compelling subject matter. Perhaps seeing this ending as a comment on the controlling nature of modern British society and a lack of magic or imagination in our culture is to take interpretation too far. However, *Monty Python and the Holy Grail*, primarily a very funny film, also succeeds in making some serious points.

Lord of the Rings

It could be argued that Peter Jackson's adaptation of the *Lord of the Rings* surpassed *Star Wars* in its impact on film audiences worldwide. In undertaking the daunting task of creating visually a world that many considered unfilmable, Jackson was largely rewarded with glowing reviews and impressive box office takings. Like *Star Wars* his films seemed to capture the imagination of audiences and their sequential release became something of an annual event. Beginning with *The Fellowship of the Ring* at Christmas 2000, continuing with *The Two Towers* in 2001 and concluding with *The Return of the King* in 2002, the films set new standards in terms of scale and special effects advances.

Designers and costume creators working on the film seemed to have turned to many visual sources connected with Grail mythology in translating the work from the page to the screen. The representations of the Elves and Lothlórien owed much to the work of the Pre-Raphaelite brotherhood and their obsession with Arthurian subject matter. The depiction of Aragorn recalled the introspection of the quest knights as he roams the wild places of Middle Earth struggling with the achievement of his own destiny to become king. As in *Excalibur*, a strong ecological theme runs through all the films as the wizard Saruman orders the destruction of the forest in his pursuit of power. Saruman is described as having a mind of metal and the severance of his magical link with nature results in the creation of a ravaged wasteland.

Obsession emerges as another key theme of the films. As Frodo follows his quest to carry the ring to Mordor and to finally destroy it in the fires of Mount Doom, its destructive powers become ever more apparent as it drains him and threatens to control him. The character and visualisation of Gollum in particular illustrates the darker side of obsession and compulsion as the ring unnaturally extends his life but twists and distorts him until he is utterly changed from his earlier more innocent incarnation of Smeagol. Although Frodo suffers on his journey he seems pre-destined to follow this quest. Gollum's ill-fated and constant search for the ring recalls the unhappy fates of the majority of the Grail knights and its divisive effects on the fellowship of the Round Table. Rendered using impressive CGI techniques, designers working on the films looked to the emaciated features of drug addicts for Gollum's physical appearance; indeed photographs of Iggy Pop provided source material in their work. His craving for the ring is shown as a painful consuming addiction.

The release of the films seemed to coincide oddly and unhappily with a series of painful events in the real world, with the terrorist attacks on the twin towers of the World Trade Center and the looming prospect of war between East and West. With George Bush's ill-considered comments on a 'crusade against terror' many people could be forgiven for fearing the imminent prospect of a new religious war. Given that the original Christian Grail stories emerged in the context of the crusades of the Middle Ages, it seemed an ironic but obviously unplanned coincidence that the *Lord of the Rings* should be released as the world seemed to teeter on the brink of another 'crusade'. However, the *Lord of the Rings* trilogy does seem to indicate the cyclical nature of human history as themes and ideas from our remote past emerge in the mainstream popular culture of the 21st century.

9

THE DA VINCI CODE

Dan Brown's 2003 novel *The Da Vinci Code* has been by far the most popular and notorious interpretation of the legend of the Holy Grail to emerge in popular culture in recent times. In many ways it has been a publishing sensation, having by 2009 sold 80 million copies worldwide. Its widespread fascination and popularity is reflected by the fact that it has also been translated into as many as 44 languages. It would appear that the subject of the Grail has captured the public imagination in the new millennium just as it did in medieval society when the French poet Chrétien de Troyes first produced the unfinished romance *Perceval* in around 1190.

The Da Vinci Code has, however, divided public and critics alike. It has both received enormous criticism for its factual inaccuracies and proved highly controversial in its depiction of the development of Christianity. Many have derided both its literary merits and poured scorn on its conclusions – but its sheer popular appeal is undeniable.

Because most readers and critics have focussed on the novel's representations of the history of the Christian Church and what Brown has claimed to be the 'true' nature of the Holy Grail, it is worth noting that *The Da Vinci Code* is essentially a crime mystery novel. What follows is a brief summary of how the crime mystery unfolds.

The novel features the central protagonist of Robert Langdon, a character whom Brown first introduces to the public in his earlier novel *Angels and Demons* (2000). American academic Robert Langdon is Professor of Religious Symbology at Harvard University and a noted world authority on the subject. *The Da Vinci Code* begins with the bizarre and mysterious murder of Jacques Sauniere, a curator at the Louvre Museum in Paris. When a strange cipher is found at the murder scene, the French police turn to Langdon for help in solving the crime. It soon becomes apparent that the French police suspect that Langdon himself may be the murderer they are looking for. Langdon is joined at the crime scene in the Louvre by a police cryptographer called Sophie Neveu, who also happens to be the granddaughter of Jacques Sauniere.

The novel later reveals that Sauniere's murder was in fact carried out by an albino monk named Silas who was working on behalf of the Roman Catholic group Opus Dei. Unknown to the police, Sauniere was the Grand Master of a secret order known as the Priory of Sion – the order in charge of protecting the secret knowledge of the location and true nature of the Holy Grail. At one point Silas forces Sauniere to tell him the location of a mysterious keystone that will lead him to the Grail. Sauniere responds by lying, and instead sends Silas to the Church of Saint Sulpice.

Eluding the police, Langdon and Neveu work together to decipher a set of clues left by Sauniere before his death. The clues lead to a painting in the Louvre behind which are hidden a key and information concerning the Priory of Sion. The pair then deduces that the key opens a safe deposit box at the Depository Bank of Zurich in Paris. Inside the deosit box they then discover a keystone in the form of a large crpytex. The keystone reputedly invented by Leonardo da Vinci, is a special device for protecting and carrying secret information. It is constructed so that if someone attempts to force it open without using the appropriate code, a small container of vinegar within the cryptex will break. Since the message inside the keystone is written on a piece of papyrus, vinegar would render it indecipherable.

Langdon and Neveu eventually seek sanctuary with Sir Leigh Teabing who is a friend of Langdon and a renowned authority on the Holy Grail. Realising the police are close behind, they escape from France onboard Teabing's personal plane. Whilst onboard they manage to open the cryptex, only to find another cryptex – it and a new riddle to unravel – inside. The riddle within the smaller cryptex reads,

> 'In London lies a knight a Pope interred.
> His labour's fruit a Holy wrath incurred.
> You seek the orb that ought to be on his tomb.
> It speaks of Rosy flesh and seeded womb.'
> (*The Da Vinci Code*, p359)

In a plot twist it emerges that Sir Teabing is not in fact an ally to Langdon and Neveu. Teabing, otherwise known as 'the Teacher', is responsible for directing Silas to the Grail. However Teabing is also responsible for leading Silas to assassinate the leaders of the Priory of Sion. In instigating a plan that would send Opus Dei in search of the Grail, Teabing was – with the help of one of the leaders of Opus Dei, Bishop Aringarosa – hoping to gain the Holy Grail for himself. Teabing's intention, it transpires, is to unlock the secret of the Grail and share knowledge with the world. He believes that the knowledge he could unlock will rewrite history and irrevocably damage the Roman Catholic Church.

Teabing steers Langdon to the Temple church in London close to Fleet Street, where a hostage scene develops between them and his collaborator Remy. The hostage scene enables Teabing to hide his identity from Langdon, whilst also obtaining the keystone.

Teabing later kills Remy and divulges Silas's location to the police.

Langdon and Neveu eventually realise that the riddle refers to the tomb of Sir Isaac Newton, which is located at Westminster Abbey. They meet Teabing at Westminster Abbey where Teabing explains his plan to reveal the secret of the Grail. Teabing claims that the ancient hidden secret of the Grail is that Mary Magdalene was the wife of Jesus Christ and that she gave birth to his child, a girl named Sarah. In Teabing's reading, Mary Magdalene herself represents the Holy Grail, because she carried the bloodline of Christ through their baby. Teabing further argues that the Priory of Sion have failed in their mission to reveal this truth to the world, and that he intends to do so himself. He tries to enlist Langdon's help in this work but Langdon refuses.

Langdon then opens and destroys the second cryptex as Teabing is arrested and taken away. Meanwhile Silas mistakenly shoots Bishop Aringarosa after trying to escape from the police, and the Bishop realises that Teabing has manipulated him.

The novel's ending sees Langdon and Neveu travel to Rosslyn chapel in Scotland where they believe the Grail is being kept. Here Neveu discovers that the guardian of the chapel is her grandmother, and that she was married to her grandfather, Jacques Sauniere. Other discoveries include that, whilst the Grail in the form of documents and the relics of Mary Magdalene had been kept at Rosslyn chapel at one point in time, they had since been moved in order to protect them. Langdon finally realises that all of the clues point back to Paris. The Grail, it transpires, is buried beneath the Louvre, hidden underneath a small pyramid located below the great inverted glass pyramid that is one of that museum's great architectural features.

Whilst many of the ideas that are explored in *The Da Vinci Code* are not in fact new, Dan Brown caused a sensation by beginning the novel with a statement declaring them to be true.

Under one of the novel's headings – which he calls 'Fact' – Brown represents the Priory of Sion as a real organisation, suggesting that in 1975 Paris's Bibliothèque Nationale had discovered documents entitled *Les Dossiers Secrets d'Henri Lobineau* (The Secret Files of Henri Lobineau) that belonged to the Priory. These documents, he contends, identify various members of the Priory through the ages, including famous figures such as Sir Isaac Newton, Victor Hugo and Leonardo da Vinci. In the same section Brown also identifies Opus Dei as a deeply devout Catholic sect whose organisational practices have been reported to include brainwashing and coercion. He also associates them with the practice of 'corporal mortification', a type of self-flagellation. Brown therefore deduces that, 'all descriptions of artwork, architecture, documents and secret rituals in this novel are accurate.'

However on his website, Brown is rather more cautious. 'While it is my belief that some of the theories discussed by these characters may have merit,' he writes, 'each individual reader must explore these characters' viewpoints and come to his or her own interpretations.' 'My hope in writing this novel', he continues, 'was that the story would serve as a catalyst and a springboard for people to discuss the important topics of faith, religion and history.' Despite seeming cautious, Brown fanned the flames of controversy when he appeared on an ABC television programme in New York and stated that the idea that the true life of Jesus was hidden by the church and distorted by them for their own ends "makes more sense to me than what I learnt as a child'.

What's more, in his novel, through the character Leigh Teabing, Brown points the finger of blame at the Roman Emperor Constantine the Great, who he says transformed Jesus from a human into a deity. The purpose of this action, Brown continues to suggest, was to strengthen and unify the Roman Empire under one God. The Church supported Constantine's decree, and in return he gave them the power to act as the established institution that all Christians had to acknowledge. This established the Church's power and control over all Roman subjects.

According to Brown, the matter of Christ's divinity was established at the Council of Nicaea in 325. The Council of Nicaea arose during Constantine's time from a dispute between different Christian factions about the true nature of the divinity of Christ. According to Brown it was a 'relatively close vote', with 218 bishops voting in favour of the unity of the Holy Trinity and 2 voting to endorse the views of the heretical priest Arius. Arius argued that Christ was younger than God, and was created as his instrument and was therefore less powerful.

Another of the arguments that Brown espouses in his novel is that the Church directed society away from matriarchal paganism towards patriarchal Christianity, and in the process demonised the sacred feminine. This, he suggests, is reflected in the witch hunts of the Middle Ages and the transformation of the character of Mary Magdalene from loyal apostle to reformed prostitute.

Mary Magdalene
Chapter 58 of *The Da Vinci Code* contains the claim that Jesus Christ was in fact married to Mary Magdalene. The novel depicts them both emerging from royal bloodlines, and as such suggests that their union would have provided Jesus with a claim to the Kingship of Israel.

Jesus was descended from King David and his son Solomon, who had built the Jewish Temple in the city of Jerusalem. Like the first King of Israel, Saul, Mary Magdalene was part of the tribe of Benjamin. Although the Bible makes no mention of this fact, Brown draws on material from the Gnostic Gospels for evidence that Jesus and Mary were married. The Gnostic Gospels are ancient Christian texts that were found in Egypt at Nag Hammadi in 1945. Brown refers to these as 'Coptic Scrolls'.

The Coptic Scrolls contain ideas and beliefs that are

divergent from Orthodox Christianity and were not included in the Bible. Many have drawn attention to one particular passage, which appears in the Gnostic Gospel of Philip:

'The companion of the Saviour is Mary Magdalene. Christ loved her more than all the disciples and used to kiss her often on her mouth. The rest of the disciples were offended by it. They said to him, "Why do you love her more than all of us?"'

However, many have argued that the teachings within Gnostic texts are in fact allegorical, and that the reference to kissing represents the passing of gnosis, or knowledge of spiritual mysteries, from one individual to another. Brown suggests that Jesus wanted Mary Magdalene to lead his church and that this wish was suppressed at a later stage by the Roman Emperor Constantine (amongst others) to suit his own purposes.

Brown also uses material from the Gnostic Gospels to assert that Christ was originally conceived of as being human, and quotes supporting material from the Gospel of Philip and the Gospel of Mary Magdalene. In constructing this argument, Brown does omit material from the Gospel of Mary Magdalene, which states that after his crucifixion, Jesus was resurrected and appeared to Mary Magdalene – thereby by asserting his divine nature. *The Da Vinci Code* endorses the view that the Holy Grail was never in fact a physical cup or vessel but is in fact a coded reference to Mary Magdalene. The novel claims that Mary Magdalene was the wife of Jesus Christ and that she became pregnant by him and had his child after the events of the crucifixion and his subsequent death. This child, a daughter, was named Sarah . In this reading the Holy Grail is a holy bloodline descending from Jesus Christ himself, and Mary is the 'chalice' that contained the bloodline. Brown argues that the French phrase '*sangrael*', meaning Holy Grail, is actually derived from an older phrase *sang real* meaning 'Holy Blood'. As mentioned earlier, this idea was developed by the authors Baigent, Lincoln and Leigh who studied a 15th century English romance in which John Hardyng uses the term '*san greal*'.

Some critics argue that this terminology may have arisen from a transcription error.

The Da Vinci Code delineates the claim that Mary Magdalene fled to France after the crucifixion of Jesus, and took refuge with the Jewish community there. This theory resonates with a legend that Mary Magdalene travelled to the fishing village of Les Saintes-Mary-de-la-Mer, the capital of the Camargue in the south of France. There are still those who celebrate the story of Mary's arrival each year on the 24th and 25th of May. This legend also contends that Mary was accompanied on her travels by an Ethiopian servant – named Sarah.

This particular story seems itself to have originated in a medieval legend designed to prove that Mary Magdalene had travelled to France, and that her bones had been placed in the abbey church St Maximin-la-Ste-Baume after her death. From there a monk from Vezelay in Burgundy purportedly transferred the bones to a shrine at Vezelay. The shrine lay on a pilgrimage trail to Santiago de Compostela, and became a great source of revenue. Later King Charles of Anjou (1226–1285) proclaimed that the relics of Mary Magdalene were still present at St Maximin-la-Ste-Baume, which has since remained popular with pilgrims.

Priory of Sion

The Da Vinci Code depicts a secret society called the Priory of Sion (Prieuré de Sion) as the guardian of the secret nature of the Holy Grail. As previously mentioned, Brown has famously claimed that the Priory of Sion is a real organisation. Chapter 37 of *The Da Vinci Code* bears evidence of this conviction, stating that the Priory of Sion was founded in 1099 after the success of the First Crusade and the capture of the holy city of Jerusalem by Western Crusaders.

The Priory was allegedly set up by Godefroi de Bouillon, one of the leaders of the First Crusade. De Bouillon established the Priory because he was aware of the true nature of the Grail and the accompanying truth about the bloodline of Mary

Magdalene and Jesus Christ. In order to support this theory, in his novel Brown describes that Godefroi founded the Priory of Sion and their military arm, the Knights Templar, in order to search for the ancient documents and relics of Mary Magdalene buried beneath the Temple of Solomon in the city of Jerusalem. According to Brown, the Templars did locate something mysterious beneath the Temple Mount, and kept it a secret in return for the support and indulgence of the Vatican, who made them wealthy and prosperous. However, when the Order of the Knights Templar was suppressed by the Pope in 1307, they are supposed to have passed their secret knowledge on to the Priory of Sion.

According to *The Da Vinci Code*, the Priory has since that time remained hidden from conventional histories but has boasted an array of world famous figures as its Grand Masters, including Leonardo da Vinci. The Priory is said to revere the sacred feminine and its aim is to revel the secret history of Jesus and Mary Magdalene when the world is ready to receive it. At any one time the Priory is said to be governed by one Grand Master and three Senechaux (officers). In *The Da Vinci Code*, the Vatican is aware of its existence and the two organisations have a hostile relationship.

Whilst *The Da Vinci Code* portrays the Priory of Sion as in fact a real organisation, it has now generally been accepted that it is in fact a hoax. The Priory of Sion was most famously brought to the public's attention by means of the bestselling book, *The Holy Blood and the Holy Grail* (1982) by Michael Baigent, Henry Linoln and Richard Leigh. Brown appears to have drawn heavily on *The Holy Blood and the Holy Grail* and in 2006 was taken to court by the authors for plagiarism. Evidence of the influence of this book is found in the name of *The Da Vinci Code*'s Grail historian Leigh Teabing – an anagram of the names 'Baigent' and 'Leigh'.

The Priory of Sion was in reality an organisation founded in the town of Annemasse in France in 1956 by a man named Pierre Plantard. Pierre Plantard co-founded the fraternal organisation with Andre Bonhomme, who acted as President whilst Plantard fulfilled the role of Secretary General. The organisation also included Armand Defago (Treasurer) and another man called Jean Deleaval (Vice-President). The Priory of Sion produced a journal known as *Circuit* and was based in Pierre Plantard's apartment. Whilst Plantard would later claim that the Priory of Sion was first founded in Jerusalem in 1099 and was an offshoot of a real Abbey of Sion located there, the group actually named themselves after a hill south of the town of Annemasse in France: Mont Sion.

Plantard invented a secret history for the organisation during the 1960s. This history claimed that the Priory protected the secret knowledge that the Merovingian Kings of France were descended from the bloodline of Jesus Christ and Mary Magdalene, and that Plantard was the rightful successor to the French crown. He focussed particularly on the 7th century Merovingian, King Dagobert II.

To substantiate these claims, Plantard and his friend Philippe de Cherisey created a number of false documents that they then planted at the Bibliothèque nationale de France in Paris. The documents were called the *Dossiers Secrets d'Henri Lobineau* (the secret dossiers of Henri Lobineau). They also created a number of forged medieval parchments that they linked to stories about Berenger Sauniere, a priest in the town of Rennes-le-Chateau, who discovered ancient parchments inside a pillar in his church. In order to further spread his dynastic claims, Plantard passed his forged documents to author Gerard de Sede, who then wrote a book based on them, *The Gold of Rennes* or *The Strange Life of Berenger Saunier, Priest of Rennes le Chateau*.

A later paperback edition of the book, *The Accursed Treasure of Rennes le Chateau*, proved popular but contained material that dated from the 19th century rather than from ancient provenance. The name of the Grand Master of the Priory of Sion in *The Da Vinci Code*, Jacques Sauniere, is a reference to the priest of Rennes-le-Chateau, Berenger

Sauniere. Gérard de Sède's *Le Trésor Maudit de Rennes-le-Château (The Accursed Treasure of Rennes le Chateau)* was read by Henry Lincoln in 1969. Lincoln later used it as the basis for books and television series exploring this conspiracy theory. Working with authors Michael Baigent and Richard Leigh, Lincoln used the forged *Dossiers Secrets* as the basis for the book *Holy Blood, Holy Grail*.

Plantard continued forging documents until 1993, when a judge investigating the activities of a multi-millionaire called Roger-Patrice Pelat was told that Plantard had claimed Pelat was a Grand Master of the Priory of Sion. When the judge ordered Plantard's residence to be searched, a number of forged documents were discovered. Plantard admitted under oath that he had fabricated everything concerning the Priory of Sion and was ordered by the court to desist from these activities.

Opus Dei

According to *The Da Vinci Code*, the ultra conservative Roman Catholic organisation Opus Dei is aware of the existence of the Priory of Sion and sends the albino monk Silas to assassinate its leaders and destroy the Holy Grail.

Opus Dei ('God's work') is a real organisation and was founded by Father Josemaría Escrivá in Spain in 1928. The organisation has grown in importance and wealth within the Roman Catholic Church since Pope John Paul II elevated it to a personal Prelature in 1982. Opus Dei founder, Father Josemaría Escrivá was canonised by Pope John Paul II in 2002. His path to sainthood is generally considered to have been extremely fast, as he died as recently as 1975. Elements of Opus Dei practices depicted by Brown such as the use of the cilice, a leather strap fitted with metal barbs and attached to the thigh, are based on reality and there has been some controversy regarding practices such as these by the organisation. Other such practices include brain washing and corporal mortification. The Opus Dei World Headquarters described in *The Da Vinci Code* is a real location based at 243 Lexington Avenue in Manhattan.

Leonardo da Vinci

According to what Dan Brown depicts in *The Da Vinci Code*, as Grand Master of the Priory of Sion, Leonardo da Vinci left a sequence of clues in his work. These apparently reveal da Vinci's reverence for the sacred feminine and his knowledge of the true nature of the Holy Grail. Paintings such as the *Mona Lisa* and *Madonna of the Rocks* are particularly suggestive of this, as is the drawing *Vitruvian Man*.

According to the character Leigh Teabing, Leonardo da Vinci makes the story of the relationship between Christ and Mary Magdalene most explicit in his fresco painting *The Last Supper*. Brown points out that there is not a single cup or chalice present on the table from which Christ and the disciples are dining. This appears to contradict the Gospel accounts of the Last Supper where Christ passed around a cup of wine and said, 'Drink of my blood'. Teabing claims that the figure who sits at the right of Christ is not in fact the Disciple John, as conventional art historians believe, but is in fact Mary Magdalene. Furthermore, Teabing also contends that da Vinci created specific clues within the painting's composition about the relationship between Christ and Mary Magdalene. Da Vinci presents the two figures, Teabing insists, in the form of a 'V' shape. This 'V' shape, he continues, is in fact a feminine symbol representing the chalice, or womb, of a woman. He also states that their silhouettes form an 'M' shape that may stand either for marriage or the name of Mary Magdalene.

Teabing also speculates that *The Last Supper* depicts the apostle Peter in the throes of an aggressive gesture, holding his hand across Mary Magdalene's throat. This, according to Teabing, also reflects Peter's jealousy found in the lost Gnostic Gospel of Mary Magdalene. Many have noted that the ideas that Teabing articulates regarding Leonardo da Vinci, Brown appears to have drawn from the book *The Templar Revelation* by Lynn Picknett and Clive Prince. Critics of Brown point out that Leonardo da Vinci chose to follow the Gospel of St John in devising his fresco. This Gospel describes the moment when the supper has finished and Christ is revealing that one of the apostles will betray him. This then is why there are no cups present on the table. This also accounts for the dramatic and unusual composition of the apostles, reeling in shock following Christ's revelation. Conventional art critics argue that the depiction of John the Evangelist as a feminine figure keeps with artistic styles of the time, and that Leonardo da Vinci also painted St John the Baptist in a notably similar style.

Rosslyn Chapel

The final section of *The Da Vinci Code* sees Robert Langdon searching for the Holy Grail in a hidden crypt beneath Rosslyn Chapel in Scotland. Rosslyn castle is sited on a volcanic plug around which flows the River Esk. The chapel, which lies south of Edinburgh, has been the source of a great deal of speculation in Grail lore. Dan Brown was particularly influenced by the novel *Rosslyn: Guardians of the Secret of the Holy Grail* when he was researching *The Da Vinci Code*. Through the character of Langdon, Brown posits that the chapel at Rosslyn was originally the site of a temple of Mithras, and that it is located on a Rose Line, another name given to a meridian line running from North to South. The suggestion is then made that the same Rose Line runs through Glastonbury, although the two locations have different compass bearings. It is from this meridian, or Rose Line, that Rosslyn is then said to take its name. However, the real origin of the name Rosslyn derives from 'Ross' meaning promontory or headland, and 'Lynn' a term that means a pool or a stream.

Through *The Da Vinci Code* Brown also puts forth the argument that Rosslyn chapel is a purposely built replica of the Temple of Solomon built in the city of Jerusalem. The history of the original temple reveals that it was destroyed by the Babylonians in around 597 BC. The Romans destroyed its successor during the Jewish revolt of AD 70. It is therefore unlikely that any plans would have been available to the builders of Rosslyn Chapel in 1446. It is now widely believed that

Rosslyn Chapel was in fact based on the choir of Glasgow Cathedral. William St Clair, who built Rosslyn Chapel, was a descendant of the St Clairs who had testified against the Templars when they went on trial at Holyrood Palace in 1309. It seems unlikely that there is a link between the Templars, the Masons and Rosslyn chapel, as many have argued.

The Star of David space that Brown depicts in *The Da Vinci Code* is a fictional invention. As yet no great subterranean chamber has been found underneath the chapel other than the expected crypt space.

The huge popular success of Dan Brown's novel led, perhaps unsurprisingly, to a major film adaptation. Released on the 19th May 2006, the film version of *The Da Vinci Code* was directed by Ron Howard and starred Tom Hanks as Robert Langdon. The film also featured Paul Bettany as the albino monk Silas, Sir Ian Mckellen as Leigh Teabing, Audrey Tatou as Sophie Neveu, Alfred Molina as Bishop Aringarosa and Jean Reno as Bezu Fache. The film encountered harsh criticism for its perceived factual inaccuracies, and there were calls from many quarters for the film to be banned or for audiences to boycott it.

At a Vatican conference held on the 28th April 2006, Archbishop Angelo Amato, secretary of the Congregation for the Doctrine of the Faith, said that *The Da Vinci Code* film was 'full of calumnies, offences and historical and theological errors'. The Archbishop requested that Roman Catholics worldwide should boycott the film. It was also poorly received by film critics and proved unpopular when shown at the Cannes film festival on the 17th May 2006. The film did however earn $230 million worldwide over its opening weekend alone. At the time of its release, this result ranked it the third most successful opening weekend for a film of all time. In 2010, *The Da Vinci Code* was ranked as the seventh most successful opening weekend of all time. It also proved to be one of the most financially successful films of 2006.

Clearly then, despite the hostile reception it received from religious groups and film critics worldwide, *The Da Vinci Code* was a huge popular hit with the general public. It is of course interesting to consider why a novel and film concerning the true nature of the Holy Grail has fascinated modern audiences. Clearly, if the plot of *The Da Vinci Code* was true, it would fundamentally influence views concerning the history and message of Christianity. In many ways it is arguable that modern audiences, like medieval audiences, are drawn to the enigmatic and secretive nature of the Grail, and that it is the mystery surrounding the Grail that makes it an enduringly popular topic.

Whether it is factually true or not, it is striking to observe that a story written as popular entertainment in around 1190 by the French poet Chrétien de Troyes has had such a dramatic and lasting cultural impact. In the wake of its first unfinished appearance, many more poets would come to attempt to solve its mysteries. In this sense, for all its dubious claims and the criticisms it has encountered as a novel, Dan Brown's *The Da Vinci Code* has continued a popular tradition that reaches back for over 800 years. It also seems likely that the Holy Grail will continue to inspire storytellers far into the future.

RESOURCES

The Holy Grail **from** *The Book of King Arthur*
By Sir Thomas Malory

CHAPTER IV

HOW THE OLD MAN BROUGHT GALAHAD TO THE SIEGE PERILOUS AND SET HIM THEREIN, AND HOW ALL THE KNIGHTS MARVELLED

The king was right glad of his words, and said unto the good man: Sir, ye be right welcome, and the young knight with you. Then the old man made the young man to unarm him, and he was in a coat of red sendel, and bare a mantle upon his shoulder that was furred with ermine, and put that upon him. And the old knight said unto the young knight: Sir, follow me. And anon he led him unto the Siege Perilous, where beside sat Sir Launcelot; and the good man lift up the cloth, and found there letters that said thus: This is the siege of Galahad, the haut prince. Sir, said the old knight, wit ye well that place is yours. And then he set him down surely in that siege. And then he said to the old man: Sir, ye may now go your way, for well have ye done that ye were commanded to do; and recommend me unto my grandsire, King Pelles, and unto my lord Petchere, and say them on my behalf, I shall come and see them as soon as ever I may. So the good man departed; and there met him twenty noble squires, and so took their horses and went their way. Then all the knights of the Table Round marvelled greatly of Sir Galahad, that he durst sit there in that Siege Perilous, and was so tender of age; and wist not from whence he came but all only by God; and said: This is he by whom the Sangreal shall be achieved, for there sat never none but he, but he were mischieved. Then Sir Launcelot beheld his son and had great joy of him. Then Bors told his fellows: Upon pain of my life this young knight shall come unto great worship. This noise was great in all the court, so that it came to the queen. Then she had marvel what knight it might be that durst adventure him to sit in the Siege Perilous. Many said unto the queen he resembled much unto Sir Launcelot. I may well suppose, said the queen, that Sir Launcelot begat him on King Pelles' daughter, by the which he was made to lie by, by enchantment, and his name is Galahad. I would fain see him, said the queen, for he must needs be a noble man, for so is his father that him begat, I report me unto all the Table Round. So when the meat was done that the king and all were risen, the king yede unto the Siege Perilous and lift up the cloth, and found there the name of Galahad; and then he shewed it unto Sir Gawaine, and said: Fair nephew, now have we among us Sir Galahad, the good knight that shall worship us all; and upon pain of my life he shall achieve the Sangreal, right as Sir Launcelot had done us to understand. Then came King Arthur unto Galahad and said: Sir, ye be welcome, for ye shall move many good knights to the quest of the Sangreal, and ye shall achieve that never knights might bring to an end. Then the king took him by the hand, and went down from the palace to shew Galahad the adventures of the stone.

CHAPTER XV

HOW SIR LAUNCELOT WAS AFORE THE DOOR OF THE
CHAMBER WHEREIN THE HOLY SANGREAL WAS

Then he enforced him mickle to undo the door. Then he listened and heard a voice which sang so sweetly that it seemed none earthly thing; and him thought the voice said: Joy and honour be to the Father of Heaven. Then Launcelot kneeled down tofore the chamber, for well wist he that there was the Sangreal within that chamber. Then said he: Fair sweet Father, Jesu Christ, if ever I did thing that pleased Thee, Lord for Thy pity never have me not in despite for my sins done aforetime, and that Thou show me something of that I seek. And with that he saw the chamber door open, and there came out a great clereness, that the house was as bright as all the torches of the world had been there. So came he to the chamber door, and would have entered. And anon a voice said to him, Flee, Launcelot, and enter not, for thou oughtest not to do it; and if thou enter thou shalt forethink it. Then he withdrew him aback right heavy. Then looked he up in the middes of the chamber, and saw a table of silver, and the holy vessel, covered with red samite, and many angels about it, whereof one held a candle of wax burning, and the other held a cross, and the ornaments of an altar. And before the holy vessel he saw a good man clothed as a priest. And it seemed that he was at the sacring of the mass. And it seemed to Launcelot that above the priest's hands were three men, whereof the two put the youngest by likeness between the priest's hands; and so he lift it up right high, and it seemed to show so to the people. And then Launcelot marvelled not a little, for him thought the priest was so greatly charged of the figure that him seemed that he should fall to the earth. And when he saw none about him that would help him, then came he to the door a great pace, and said: Fair Father Jesu Christ, ne take it for no sin though I help the good man which hath great need of help. Right so entered he into the chamber, and came toward the table of silver; and when he came nigh he felt a breath, that him thought it was intermeddled with fire, which smote him so sore in the visage that him thought it brent his visage; and therewith he fell to the earth, and had no power to arise, as he that was so araged, that had lost the power of his body, and his hearing, and his seeing. Then felt he many hands about him, which took him up and bare him out of the chamber door, without any amending of his swoon, and left him there, seeming dead to all people. So upon the morrow when it was fair day they within were arisen, and found Launcelot lying afore the chamber door. All they marvelled how that he came in, and so they looked upon him, and felt his pulse to wit whether there were any life in him; and so they found life in him, but he might not stand nor stir no member that he had. And so they took him by every part of the body, and bare him into a chamber, and laid him in a rich bed, far from all folk; and so he lay four days. Then the one said he was on live, and the other said, Nay. In the name of God, said an old man, for I do you verily to wit he is not dead, but he is so full of life as the mightiest of you all; and therefore I counsel you that he be well kept till God send him life again.

The Holy Grail
By Alfred Lord Tennyson

From noiseful arms, and acts of prowess done
In tournament or tilt, Sir Percivale,
Whom Arthur and his knighthood called The Pure,
Had passed into the silent life of prayer,
Praise, fast, and alms; and leaving for the cowl
The helmet in an abbey far away
  From Camelot, there, and not long after, died.

  And one, a fellow-monk among the rest,
Ambrosius, loved him much beyond the rest,

And honoured him, and wrought into his heart
A way by love that wakened love within,
To answer that which came: and as they sat
Beneath a world-old yew-tree, darkening half
The cloisters, on a gustful April morn
That puffed the swaying branches into smoke
Above them, ere the summer when he died
The monk Ambrosius questioned Percivale:

'O brother, I have seen this yew-tree smoke,
Spring after spring, for half a hundred years:
For never have I known the world without,
Nor ever strayed beyond the pale: but thee,
When first thou camest – such a courtesy
Spake through the limbs and in the voice – I knew
For one of those who eat in Arthur's hall;
For good ye are and bad, and like to coins,
Some true, some light, but every one of you
Stamped with the image of the King; and now
Tell me, what drove thee from the Table Round,
My brother? was it earthly passion crost?'

'Nay,' said the knight; 'for no such passion mine.
But the sweet vision of the Holy Grail
Drove me from all vainglories, rivalries,
And earthly heats that spring and sparkle out
Among us in the jousts, while women watch
Who wins, who falls; and waste the spiritual strength
Within us, better offered up to Heaven.'

To whom the monk: 'The Holy Grail! – I trust
We are green in Heaven's eyes; but here too much
We moulder – as to things without I mean –
Yet one of your own knights, a guest of ours,
Told us of this in our refectory,
But spake with such a sadness and so low

We heard not half of what he said. What is it?
The phantom of a cup that comes and goes?'

'Nay, monk! what phantom?' answered Percivale.
'The cup, the cup itself, from which our Lord
Drank at the last sad supper with his own.
This, from the blessed land of Aromat –
    After the day of darkness, when the dead
Went wandering o'er Moriah – the good saint
Arimathaean Joseph, journeying brought
To Glastonbury, where the winter thorn
Blossoms at Christmas, mindful of our Lord.
And there awhile it bode; and if a man
Could touch or see it, he was healed at once,
By faith, of all his ills. But then the times
Grew to such evil that the holy cup
Was caught away to Heaven, and disappeared.'

    To whom the monk: 'From our old books I know
That Joseph came of old to Glastonbury,
And there the heathen Prince, Arviragus,
Gave him an isle of marsh whereon to build;
And there he built with wattles from the marsh
A little lonely church in days of yore,
For so they say, these books of ours, but seem
Mute of this miracle, far as I have read.
But who first saw the holy thing today?'

    'A woman,' answered Percivale, 'a nun,
And one no further off in blood from me
Than sister; and if ever holy maid
With knees of adoration wore the stone,
A holy maid; though never maiden glowed,
But that was in her earlier maidenhood,
With such a fervent flame of human love,

Which being rudely blunted, glanced and shot
Only to holy things; to prayer and praise
She gave herself, to fast and alms. And yet,
Nun as she was, the scandal of the Court,
Sin against Arthur and the Table Round,
And the strange sound of an adulterous race,
Across the iron grating of her cell
Beat, and she prayed and fasted all the more.

'And he to whom she told her sins, or what
Her all but utter whiteness held for sin,
A man wellnigh a hundred winters old,
Spake often with her of the Holy Grail,
A legend handed down through five or six,
And each of these a hundred winters old,
From our Lord's time. And when King Arthur made
His Table Round, and all men's hearts became
Clean for a season, surely he had thought
That now the Holy Grail would come again;
But sin broke out. Ah, Christ, that it would come,
And heal the world of all their wickedness!

The Sancgreal
By Dante Gabriel Rossetti

It chanced, when Lancelot du Lake
    Had freed from durance vile
The fairest lady in the land,
    He journeyed on awhile,

Until King Pelles spied the knight,
    Whose castle stood hard by,
And begged him to alight and share
    His hospitality.

So courteously and graciously
    The twain passed through the gate,
Then sat within the banquet hall,
    The viands to await.

But lo! through window opened wide,
    Without or voice or sound,
A gentle dove came gliding in,
    And floated round and round.

Within her beak a censer hung
    Cast in pure molten gold,
Whence clouds of fragrance issued forth
    Which o'er the table rolled.

It seemed as Araby the blest,
    And every spicy isle,
Had garnered all their treasures up,
    To waft them there the while.

And forthwithal upon the board
    All kinds of meats were spread,
And drinks that might the palate please
    Were likewise furnishèd.

A damsel passing fair and young,
    Most beauteous to behold,
Came gliding in – betwixt her hands
    She bare a vase of gold.

And thereunto the King kneeled down,
    Devoutly and with grace,
To say his prayers, as also did
    Each soul within the place.

Then spake Sir Lancelot du Lake
    And askèd of the King,
'What may this mean? I pray you tell.'
    'This is the richest thing,'

Replied King Pelles, 'that a man
    Can own, alive or dead;
E'en the Round Table, when this comes,
    Shall be abolishèd.

'And wit thou well, thou here hast seen
    The holy Sangreal –
The blessed gift – the cherished hope
    Sought for and prayed of all.'

In after years when Lancelot
    Had wedded sweet Elaine,
King Pelles' child, within those walls,
    The wonder happed again.

For Lancelot's nephew, young Sir Bors,
    To Corben Castle rode,
And in the banquet-hall he saw
    Elaine, just where she stood,

Her baby on her arm; and when
    She said the lovely boy
Was Lancelot's child, he kneelèd down
    And wept for very joy,

And prayed to God, that when the child
    To years of manhood grew,
He might prove worthy of his sire,
    As brave a knight and true.

Then through the window opened wide,
    Without or voice or sound,
A gentle dove came gliding in,
    And floated round and round.

Within her beak a censer hung
    Formed of pure molten gold,
Whence clouds of fragrance issued forth,
    Which o'er the table rolled.

It seemed as Araby the blest,
    And every spicy isle,
Had garnered all their treasures up
    To waft them there awhile.

And forthwithal upon the board
    All kinds of meats were spread,
And drinks that might the palate please
    Were also furnishèd.

A damsel passing fair and young,
    Most beauteous to behold,
Came gliding in, betwixt her hands
    Bearing a vase of gold.

She spake, 'This babe Sir Galahad,
    Sir Bors, I bid you wit,
In future on Siege Perilous
    As knight shall surely sit –

'A nobler knight than is his sire' –
    Her words rang through the hall –
'For as he lives, he surely shall
    Achieve the Sancgreal.'

She vanished then. As of afore,
    King Pelles spoke out loud:
'No knight shall win, or honour have,
    Save he that loveth God.

'Be he a knight of high degree,
    Or be he e'er so brave,
An he nor love nor feareth God,
    No honour shall he have.'

Replied Sir Bors, 'Within these halls
    (I wot not what they mean)
Most strange and weird adventures hap,
    And wondrous sights are seen.
I will be shriven with good will
    And be confessèd clean.'

So was he shriven of his sins,
    And in the dead of night
Most marvellous adventures happed,
    Too lengthy here to write.

When morning broke, to Camelot
    He spurred his gallant steed;
For Arthur had returned from France
    Victorious, and decreed

That feasts and tournaments be held
    Upon that very day,
And all his knights at Table Round
    Should sit in full array.

But when uncovered was the siege
    Hight Perilous, behold,
The name of young Sir Galahad
    Shone forth in molten gold.

But no one at the Table wot
    Who Galahad might be,
Till long years afterward he came
    Out from the nunnery

Where holy women reared the child
    Till he to manhood grew,
And taught him to be good and wise,
    Noble, and brave, and true.

At Pentecost, he having first
    Performed the holy rite,
On bended knee he begged to be
    Installèd as a knight.

Sir Lancelot surveyed the youth,
    And found him passing fair,
With limbs well knit, of stature tall,
    Graceful beyond compare.

He struck him with his sword, and said,
    'Sir Galahad, arise!
God grant the virtue ne'er may fade
    Now shining through your eyes!'

Sir Galahad then hasted forth,
    To joust withouten shield;
He broke their spears, he threw the knights
    Save twain who would not yield.

He then unhorsed, unlaced him helm
    At Guinever's request,
Who, looking on his visage, spake,
    'No marvel he is best

'At jousting and at holy prayer;
　　　For, as you plainly see,
His face and mien bespeak him sprung
　　　From true nobility.'

Then all to the great minster sped
　　　To offer evensong,
King, Queen, the knights of Table Round,
　　　With all the motley throng.

Then back to Camelot to sup,
　　　Where in the lofty hall,
Each sitting as toforehand, lo!
　　　This marvel did befall:

The thunder growled, and cracked ahead
　　　As though the walls would rive.
Each knight made sign of cross, as though
　　　The priest had stood to shrive.

But in the midst of crash and blast
　　　A sunbeam entered there,
By seven times brighter than the day,
　　　When day is bright and clear.

It shed such lustre over all,
　　　Each scanned his neighbour o'er;
And each seemed fairer in that light
　　　Than e'er he seemed before.

No word was spoke, no sound was made,
　　　As they all dumb had been:
The holy Grail in white samite
　　　Came softly gliding in.

And as afore the hall was filled
      With perfumes where it moved,
And every knight had meats and drinks
      As each one wished and loved.

As quickly as it glided in,
      It quick evanishèd;
None knew from whence or whitherward
      The holy vision fled.

King Arthur rose with reverence,
      Bowing full low his head:
'Thank Jesu Christ our Lord for this
      So precious boon,' he said.

Then up and spake Gawaine, 'I vow
      By all I hold most dear,
In quest of this most holy Grail,
      To wander for a year.

'And eke a day nor e'er return
      Until it reappear
Unto my longing eyes more bright
      And openly than here!'

Then rose up all the knights around,
      And vowed, with one accord,
With heart and soul to join the quest,
      For love of Christ their Lord.

King Arthur spake with troubled mien,
      'Alas! Gawaine, Gawaine!
With this avow and promise made,
      Ye have me well nigh slain.

'Alas! this morn I held secure
    A band so brave and true,
The fairest fellowship on earth
    That knighthood ever knew.

'Ye have bereft me of this band.
    Alas! it grieves me sore;
For when they once depart from hence,
    I ne'er shall meet them more.

'For many in the quest will die –
    Those that I loved so well.
How close I held them to my heart,
    No words of mine can tell.

'And thus it now forthinketh me,
    I fain for grief would die;
For 'twas an old, old usage
    To have their company.'

This spake he, with the gathering tears
    Slow trembling in his eyes,
Fresh from his o'ercharged heart, so full
    Of loving memories.

Next morn, the band of gallant knights
    Through the great minster pass,
And kneel below the altar stair
    To celebrate the mass.

And then 'to horse!' The eager crowd
    Are gathering far and near;
Maidens forlorn and gentlefolk
    With wistful eyes are there:

The rich, the poor, the camp, the court,
　　Arthur and Guinever;
They bid farewell with many a sob
　　And many a bitter tear.

They mount, they ride, their glittering plumes
　　Are waving in the wind;
Ah! what remains save aching hearts
　　To those they leave behind?

Sir Galahad, A Christmas Mystery
By William Morris

It is the longest night in all the year,
　　Near on the day when the Lord Christ was born;
Six hours ago I came and sat down here,
　　And ponder'd sadly, wearied and forlorn.

The winter wind that pass'd the chapel door,
　　Sang out a moody tune, that went right well
With mine own thoughts: I look'd down on the floor,
　　Between my feet, until I heard a bell

Sound a long way off through the forest deep,
　　And toll on steadily; a drowsiness
Came on me, so that I fell half asleep,
　　As I sat there not moving: less and less

I saw the melted snow that hung in beads
　　Upon my steel-shoes; less and less I saw
Between the tiles the bunches of small weeds:
　　Heartless and stupid, with no touch of awe

Upon me, half-shut eyes upon the ground,
    I thought: O Galahad! the days go by,
Stop and cast up now that which you have found,
    So sorely you have wrought and painfully.

Night after night your horse treads down alone
    The sere damp fern, night after night you sit
Holding the bridle like a man of stone,
    Dismal, unfriended: what thing comes of it?

And what if Palomydes also ride,
    And over many a mountain and bare heath
Follow the questing beast with none beside?
    Is he not able still to hold his breath

With thoughts of Iseult? doth he not grow pale
    With weary striving, to seem best of all
To her, 'as she is best,' he saith? to fail
    Is nothing to him, he can never fall.

For unto such a man love-sorrow is
    So dear a thing unto his constant heart,
That even if he never win one kiss,
    Or touch from Iseult, it will never part.

And he will never know her to be worse
    Than in his happiest dreams he thinks she is:
Good knight, and faithful, you have 'scaped the curse
    In wonderful-wise; you have great store of bliss.

Yea, what if Father Launcelot ride out,
    Can he not think of Guenevere's arms, round
Warm and lithe, about his neck, and shout
    Till all the place grows joyful with the sound?

And when he lists can often see her face,
   And think, 'Next month I kiss you, or next week,
And still you think of me': therefore the place
   Grows very pleasant, whatsoever he seek.

But me, who ride alone, some carle shall find
   Dead in my arms in the half-melted snow,
When all unkindly with the shifting wind,
   The thaw comes on at Candlemas: I know

Indeed that they will say: 'This Galahad
   If he had lived had been a right good knight;
Ah! poor chaste body!' but they will be glad,
   Not most alone, but all, when in their sight

That very evening in their scarlet sleeves
   The gay-dress'd minstrels sing; no maid will talk
Of sitting on my tomb, until the leaves,
   Grown big upon the bushes of the walk,

East of the Palace-pleasaunce, make it hard
   To see the minster therefrom: well-a-day!
Before the trees by autumn were well bared,
   I saw a damozel with gentle play,

Within that very walk say last farewell
   To her dear knight, just riding out to find
(Why should I choke to say it?) the Sangreal,
   And their last kisses sunk into my mind,

Yea, for she stood lean'd forward on his breast,
   Rather, scarce stood; the back of one dear hand,
That it might well be kiss'd, she held and press'd
   Against his lips; long time they stood there, fann'd

By gentle gusts of quiet frosty wind,
   Till Mador de la porte a-going by,
And my own horsehoofs roused them; they untwined,
   And parted like a dream. In this way I,

With sleepy face bent to the chapel floor,
   Kept musing half asleep, till suddenly
A sharp bell rang from close beside the door,
   And I leapt up when something pass'd me by,

Shrill ringing going with it, still half blind
   I stagger'd after, a great sense of awe
At every step kept gathering on my mind,
   Thereat I have no marvel, for I saw

One sitting on the altar as a throne,
   Whose face no man could say he did not know,
And though the bell still rang, he sat alone,
   With raiment half blood-red, half white as snow.

Right so I fell upon the floor and knelt,
   Not as one kneels in church when mass is said,
But in a heap, quite nerveless, for I felt
   The first time what a thing was perfect dread.

But mightily the gentle voice came down:
   'Rise up, and look and listen, Galahad,
Good knight of God, for you will see no frown
   Upon my face; I come to make you glad.

'For that you say that you are all alone,
   I will be with you always, and fear not
You are uncared for, though no maiden moan
   Above your empty tomb; for Launcelot,

'He in good time shall be my servant too,
    Meantime, take note whose sword first made him knight,
And who has loved him alway, yea, and who
    Still trusts him alway, though in all men's sight,

'He is just what you know, O Galahad,
    This love is happy even as you say,
But would you for a little time be glad,
    To make ME sorry long, day after day?

'Her warm arms round his neck half throttle ME,
    The hot love-tears burn deep like spots of lead,
Yea, and the years pass quick: right dismally
    Will Launcelot at one time hang his head;

'Yea, old and shrivell'd he shall win my love.
    Poor Palomydes fretting out his soul!
Not always is he able, son, to move
    His love, and do it honour: needs must roll

'The proudest destrier sometimes in the dust,
    And then 'tis weary work; he strives beside
Seem better than he is, so that his trust
    Is always on what chances may betide;

'And so he wears away, my servant, too,
    When all these things are gone, and wretchedly
He sits and longs to moan for Iseult, who
    Is no care now to Palomydes: see,

'O good son, Galahad, upon this day,
    Now even, all these things are on your side,
But these you fight not for; look up, I say,
    And see how I can love you, for no pride

'Closes your eyes, no vain lust keeps them down.
　　See now you have ME always; following
That holy vision, Galahad, go on,
　　Until at last you come to ME to sing

'In Heaven always, and to walk around
　　The garden where I am.' He ceased, my face
And wretched body fell upon the ground;
　　And when I look'd again, the holy place

Was empty; but right so the bell again
　　Came to the chapel-door, there entered
Two angels first, in white, without a stain,
　　And scarlet wings, then, after them, a bed

Four ladies bore, and set it down beneath
　　The very altar-step, and while for fear
I scarcely dared to move or draw my breath,
　　Those holy ladies gently came a-near,

And quite unarm'd me, saying: 'Galahad,
　　Rest here awhile and sleep, and take no thought
Of any other thing than being glad;
　　Hither the Sangreal will be shortly brought,

'Yet must you sleep the while it stayeth here.'
　　Right so they went away, and I, being weary,
Slept long and dream'd of Heaven: the bell comes near,
　　I doubt it grows to morning. Miserere!

*Enter Two Angels in white, with scarlet wings; also, Four
Ladies in gowns of red and green; also an Angel, bearing in his
hands a surcoat of white, with a red cross.*

AN ANGEL

O servant of the high God, Galahad!
   Rise and be arm'd: the Sangreal is gone forth
Through the great forest, and you must be had
   Unto the sea that lieth on the north:

There shall you find the wondrous ship wherein
   The spindles of King Solomon are laid,
And the sword that no man draweth without sin,
   But if he be most pure: and there is stay'd,

Hard by, Sir Launcelot, whom you will meet
   In some short space upon that ship: first, though,
Will come here presently that lady sweet,
   Sister of Percival, whom you well know,

And with her Bors and Percival: stand now,
   These ladies will to arm you.
FIRST LADY, *putting on the hauberk*
   Galahad,
That I may stand so close beneath your brow,
   Margaret of Antioch, am glad.

SECOND LADY, *girding him with the sword.*
That I may stand and touch you with my hand,
   O Galahad, I, Cecily, am glad.
THIRD LADY, *buckling on the spurs.*
That I may kneel while up above you stand,
   And gaze at me, O holy Galahad,

I, Lucy, am most glad.
FOURTH LADY, *putting on the basnet.*
   O gentle knight,
   That you bow down to us in reverence,

We are most glad, I, Katherine, with delight
    Must needs fall trembling.
ANGEL, *putting on the crossed surcoat.*
    Galahad, we go hence,

For here, amid the straying of the snow,
    Come Percival's sister, Bors, and Percival.
The Four Ladies carry out the bed,
and all go but Galahad.

GALAHAD

How still and quiet everything seems now:
    They come, too, for I hear the horsehoofs fall.

Enter Sir Bors, Sir Percival *and* his Sister.

Fair friends and gentle lady, God you save!
    A many marvels have been here to-night;
Tell me what news of Launcelot you have,
    And has God's body ever been in sight?

SIR BORS.

Why, as for seeing that same holy thing,
    As we were riding slowly side by side,
An hour ago, we heard a sweet voice sing,
    And through the bare twigs saw a great light glide,

With many-colour'd raiment, but far off;
    And so pass'd quickly: from the court nought good;
Poor merry Dinadan, that with jape and scoff
    Kept us all merry, in a little wood

Was found all hack'd and dead: Sir Lionel
    And Gauwaine have come back from the great quest,

Just merely shamed; and Lauvaine, who loved well
    Your father Launcelot, at the king's behest

Went out to seek him, but was almost slain,
    Perhaps is dead now; everywhere
The knights come foil'd from the great quest, in vain;
    In vain they struggle for the vision fair.

BIBLIOGRAPHY

Ackroyd, Peter, *Blake*, London: Minerva, 1995

Ashe, Geoffrey, *Arthur: The Dream of a Golden Age*, London: Thames & Hudson, 1990

Baigent, Michael, Leigh, Richard, Lincoln, Henry, *The Holy Blood and the Holy Grail*, London: Arrow Books, 1982

Bair, Deirdre, *Jung: A Biography*, London: Little, Brown, 2004

Barber, Richard, *The Holy Grail*, London: Allen Lane, 2004

Barber, Richard, *King Arthur: Hero and Legend*, Woodbridge: Boydell Press, 1961

Baxter, John, *George Lucas: A Biography*, London: HarperCollins, 1999

Berthelot, Anne, *King Arthur: Chivalry and Legend*, London: Thames & Hudson, 1996

Boorman, John, *Adventures of a Suburban Boy*, London: Faber and Faber, 2003

Campbell, Joseph, *The Hero With a Thousand Faces*, New York: Pantheon Books, 1949

Campbell, Joseph, *The Masks of God: Creative Mythology*, London, Secker & Warburg, 1968

Cookson, Linda and Loughrey, Bryan, *Critical Essays on The Waste Land*, Harlow: Longman, 1988

Cope, Julian, *The Modern Antiquarian*, London: Thorsons, 1998

Dames, Michael, *Merlin and Wales*, London: Thames & Hudson, 2002

Devereux, Paul, *Stone Age Soundtracks* London: Vega, 2001

Eliot, T. S., *Selected Poems*, London: Faber and Faber, 1954

Green, Miranda, *The Gods of the Celts*, Stroud: Sutton, 1986

Hamilton, Claire, *Arthurian Tradition*, London: Hodder & Stoughton, 2000

John, David, *Star Wars: The Power of Myth*, London: Dorling Kindersley, 1999

Laidler, Keith, *The Head of God: The Lost Treasures of the Templars*, London: Weidenfeld & Nicolson, 1998

Lynch, Frances, *Megalithic Tombs and Long Barrows in Britain*, Princes Risborough: Shire Publications,1997

Macrae, Alisdair, *York Notes on The Waste Land*, Harlow: Longman, 1993

Mann, Nicholas R., *The Isle of Avalon*, Bridgewater: Green Magic, 1996

Matthews, John, *The Elements of the Grail Tradition*, Shaftesbury: Element, 1990

Matthews, John, *The Grail*, London: Thames & Hudson, 1981

Mavromataki, Maria, *Greek Mythology and Religion*, Athens: Haitalis, 1997

Scavone, Daniel C., *Joseph of Arimathea, the Holy Grail and the Turin Shroud*, Bloomington: University of Indiana Press, 1996

Sturgis, Matthew, *Aubrey Beardsley*, London: HarperCollins, 1998

Tickner, Lisa, *Rossetti*, London: Tate Publishing, 2003

Waters, Bill and Harrison, Martin, *Burne-Jones*, London: Barrie & Jenkins, 1973

White, T. H., *The Once and Future King*, London: HarperCollins, 1996

Wilson, Ian, *The Turin Shroud*, London:Victor Gollancz, 1978

WEBSITES

www.bbc.co.uk/history/archaeology
www.megalithic.co.uk
www.britannia.com/history/h12.html
www.geocities.com/branwaedd/hbindex.html
www.rochester.edu/camelot/cphome.stm (University of Rochester site
   – good links to Arthurian texts and sites)
www.arthuriana.co.uk
www.legends.dm.net/kingarthur
www.greatdreams.com/arthur.htm
www.danbrown.com (Dan Brown homepage)
www.jcf.org (Joseph Campbell homepage)
www.cennectotel.com/rennes (Rennes-le-Chateau homepage)
www.shroud.com (Turin Shroud homepage)
www.vatican.va (Vatican homepage)

INDEX